THE COMPLETE
PEKINGESE

Liz Stannard

Howell Book House

HOWELL
BOOK
HOUSE

New York

HOWELL BOOK HOUSE
A Macmillan Company
1633 Broadway
New York, NY 10019

MACMILLAN is a registered trademark of Macmillan, Inc.

ISBN 1-58245-081-1

Library of Congress Cataloging-in-Publication Data
available on request

Manufactured in Hong Kong

10 9 8 7 6 5 4 3 2 1

ACKNOWLEDGEMENTS

As I am one of those people who find it hard to delegate, I have written this book completely without help so, therefore, have nobody else to blame if there are any errors.

Without the help of my non-doggy friend, Linda, who typed every word, I would probably still be writing now – so grateful thanks to her. Thanks also to Val who has written many books and encouraged me to finally get started and keep at it.

Thanks must also go to my husband Paul, who has had to live with me during a slightly hysterical few months – on top of everything else, it could not have been easy.

Hopefully, it has been worth it. If, after reading the book, you want to be owned by a Pekingese, I will have achieved my aim.

Contents

INTRODUCTION

It has been ten years since the last Pekingese book was written by breed specialists on either side of the Atlantic and in that time the breed itself has altered slightly due to fashionable trends and new people have come into the breed.

I hope this book will give you an insight into the unique character of this Oriental breed, whether you have just become a first-time owner of a dog who is, hopefully, going to be a companion for many years, or whether you have started showing and want to know more about the history of the breed and the famous names that have gone before.

Britain has always been the stronghold of the breed although numbers at shows have decreased dramatically in the last fifteen years. It is difficult to know if this is due to increased costs or whether people do not have the determination to carry on if, at first, they do not win. It is certainly a reflection on our society that everyone wants to be an instant winner, an instant judge and an instant expert,

and few are willing to serve an apprenticeship, which was the rule for those early pioneers of the breed.

There are now top winning dogs in the United States, Scandinavia and in many parts of Europe, and all those who care about the Pekingese should seek to improve the breed in terms of conformation and temperament. The search for perfection should be on-going.

Those of us who are owned by Pekingese often think we already have the perfect dog. This may be a house pet who sits there begging for a tidbit with that appealing look, or a show dog winning his first major award, giving that haughty look to the others down the line.

When I look into the faces of some of my Pekingese, I still get that goose-bump feeling. To me they are so beautiful – how can anyone say they are ugly!

Obviously, the breed has changed since the early imports. Pekingese tend to be bigger, and, in some cases, they are too big. They have flatter faces, but they are able to breathe without problems. They also have a lot more coat, much more than the Breed Standard calls for. However, underneath it all, beats the heart of a lion, filled with courage and intelligence, and with such faithfulness that, once you have owned a Pekingese, you will never want to be without one.

If you are just thinking of owning your first Peke, go for it; you will never regret it. Who knows, in thirty years time, you might end up like me, starting with one dog and ending up with a large kennel of top winners, known all over the world, with friends everywhere, and writing a book – all through the love of a little Oriental dog!

Ch. Shiarita Bobbie's Girl.

1 *ORIGINS*

The origin of some breeds is clear, of others definitely murky. That of the Pekingese is lost in the mists of time, so ancient is the breed of lion dogs. The myths of the breed's origins are like fairytales. There are many mentions of dogs in Chinese manuscripts; some mention a small dog, some a short-faced dog. We can read of the Chinese Emperor in about AD 1680 who decided dogs were much more intelligent than human beings and that this should be recognised, so he ordered that all his dogs should hold exalted ranks and wear the appropriate hats, and all the bitches in his kennel should wear ladies' hats according to their husband's rank!

There are many stories of small dogs who held candles for the Emperor or who sat by his side and barked and made people respectful. As the years passed, these small dogs became a palace breed and then the Imperial dog of China.

Why the lion dog? The name was not only due to their appearance, but to the fact that these special dogs were believed to be representations of the lions which Buddha made from his fingers.

WAR WITH CHINA
During 1860 the British and French were at war with China. Troops advanced on the Summer Palace. The Emperor and court fled. It is supposed that the Emperor's aunt had been left behind and that she had committed suicide, but with her were five dogs left alive, dogs of beauty, the lion dogs. The smallest, a fawn and white later called Looty, who travelled in General Dunne's forage cap, was presented to Queen Victoria. About three years old when he came to England in 1861, he died in 1872. There is no evidence of him living with the Queen. In letters, HRH Princess Louise, Duchess of Argyle, did remember the dog, but said

he was not a companion of the Queen and must have lived in the kennels in Windsor Great Park.

A RARE BREED

These rare dogs could be bought in China, but seemingly not easily, and usually by illegal methods. The Chinese stole them and sold them for a good price to Europeans, stole them again and resold them, or kept them and claimed the reward. We know of the different types and colours from written evidence which tells of rich chestnut brown with black markings, and fawn and white. One, belonging to an English girl who lived nearly all of her life in China, was a beautiful little sleeve dog, yellow and white with a lovely long coat, weighing about two and a half to three pounds – she called him a Chinese Pug. The Empress's favourite was black with a little white. Black and tan was another colour, as was red.

The early Pekes sent to England were bred together but nobody bothered about pedigrees, nor did the puppies seem popular. In 1893 Captain Loftus Allen, a sea captain, bought for his wife a dog later called Pekin Peter who, in 1894, became the first Peke to be shown in England at the Chester Show. He was followed in 1896 by Pekin Prince and Pekin Princess, both blacks weighing eight pounds and six pounds respectively, slightly more than previous imports who had mostly been what we would now call sleeves.

Mrs Allen went to China on a number of occasions with her husband and was able to buy dogs from a Chinese dealer, although how he obtained them is unclear, as punishment for stealing them was still death.

EARLY IMPORTS

Mrs Allen did some breeding, her most famous dog being Pekin Pretty, but her Pekes were rarely seen in the show ring apart from the occasional dog being shown under the name of a Pekingese Pug or Tientseien Spaniel. Little seems

The Emperor's court in Peking. The Pekingese is a particolour, photographed approx. 1890.

to have happened until 1896 when two more Pekes arrived, Ah Cum and Mimosa. Mr and Mrs Douglas Murray, who imported them, had them smuggled out of China in a crate containing deer. Ah Cum was exhibited at the Royal Aquarium Pet Dog Show in May 1898 where he was beaten by Pekin Prince. The breeding of Pekes, with Ah Cum as sire, was the start of the Pekingese becoming the fashionable breed in England. Visitors to the British Museum Natural History Section at Tring, Hertfordshire, today can see Ah Cum, shoulder height 20 cm (8 ins), born around 1895, died January 1905, presented by Mrs Douglas Murray. There he stands, the foundation of the famous Palace Kennel, considered the patriarch of the breed in England, being responsible for many of the early Champions. He was said to be beautiful in colour and carriage, light-boned with straight forelegs, his coat comparatively light and his tail more like a tuft than a plume. He was reputed to weigh five pounds but, having seen his stuffed body, he looks to me as though he was heavier.

Also on display are Palace Yo Tei with her pedigree KCSB No. 1407M. She died at four years, her sire and dam both being by Ah Cum. With Palace Yo Tei is Li-Tzu, an imported bitch shown by the Hon. Mrs L. Carnegie. Li-Tzu was black with a white shirt front and socks. Further dogs were imported and,

of the original five, two were given by Sir George Fitzroy to his relations, the Duke and Duchess of Richmond and Gordon. Nothing is known of these two but presumably they must have bred on as the Duke and Duchess's son, Lord Algernon Gordon-Lennox, established with his wife the famous Goodwood strain.

FIRST BREEDERS

The breed really took off after the Gordon-Lennoxes met up with the Douglas Murrays. The Goodwood stock needed new blood and when Ah Cum was mated to two Goodwood bitches, Meh and Queenie, the resulting puppy from Meh became the breed's first Champion Goodwood Lo. The breed became more popular in Britain, as more dogs were imported and Pekingese puppies changed hands for quite high prices compared to other breeds.

George Brown, a Consular official in China, returned home with some Pekes he had bred out there and mated one of his bitches, Pinkee (whose sire was unknown), to Ah Cum. One of the puppies, Tai Tai, was sold to Mrs Gray and she was mated to Pekin Paul (Pekin Prince ex Pekin Princess) and, from the resulting litter, came the first bitch Champion Gia Gia. Gia Gia is in most extended pedigrees today as her grandson was Ch. Chu-Erh of Alderbourne who was the founder of a dynasty.

The Manchu kennel was also behind Sutherland Avenue Ouen Teu T'ang who was used extensively at a lot in the early days.

In 1898 the Japanese Spaniel Club drew up the first Pekingese points. In 1900 new points were drawn up by Lady Gordon-Lennox, Mrs Douglas Murray and Mrs Albert Gray. A club was formed that year, the Japanese and Other Asiatic Spaniels Association, and Lady Gordon-Lennox became the president.

During the Boxer uprising, the allied troops entered the Forbidden City itself and the Dowager Empress fled with the court and all of the Palace dogs.

A British Army officer was able to acquire two Pekes in return for the safe passage out of Peking of one of the palace hierarchy.

One of these dogs was Boxer, a larger, heavier dog than previous imports. He was probably one of the last imports from China.

IN THE SHOW RING

In 1901 Pekes were no longer classed as a foreign breed and were allowed Challenge Certificates at leading Championship shows.

In that year Goodwood Lo first appeared in the ring, winning the Over Ten Pound class at Crystal Palace. At the same show, Ah Cum, his sire, was placed third.

The year 1904 was important. The Pekingese Club was formed from a division of the Japanese and Other Asiatic Spaniels Association, again with Lady Gordon-Lennox as President. Two years earlier saw the awarding of the first Pekingese CC which went to Goodwood Lo, owned by Mrs Douglas Murray. He won his second later that year.

During the same year Gia Gia, owned by Gertrude, Lady Decies, won two CCs and so both she and Lo went to Crufts the following year hoping to win their third to become the breed's first Champion. But it was not to be for

Queen Alexandra's Pekingese, Fluospar, modelled by Fabergé. This forms part of the Royal Collection.

either of them as, even though Lo won the Mixed Open Class, he did not win the CC. In May at Crystal Palace he won his third and became the breed's first Champion. Later that year Gia Gia also won her third CC after winning the Open Class over ten pounds. Presumably both of these first two Champions were over the weight limit of 10 lbs (4.5 kg) set by the Pekingese Club at that time. This was altered for a while to 18 lbs (8 kg) and then scrapped altogether. This was probably one of the reasons for the formation of the Pekin Palace Dog Association in 1908 which re-set the weight limit at 10 lbs (4.5 kg).

Another famous dog was Goodwood Chun who gave his name to a particular shade of red which was similar to chestnut with a coppery sheen. This colour is not seen nowadays, as the most popular colour is fawn which carries a much heavier coat and looks more glamorous, although glamour is not mentioned anywhere in the Breed Standard. Chun won BOB at Crufts in 1905.

Those early kennel names of Goodwood, Palace, Pekin and Manchu all but disappeared after the First World War but we can trace back to the Manchus through the most famous kennel name of the early 20th century, the Alderbournes.

THE ALDERBOURNE KENNEL

The numbers of Pekingese at shows increased rapidly in those days from ones and twos to the fantastic number of 213 at the Ladies Kennel Association in 1906. It was at this show that Chu-Erh of Alderbourne first appeared.

Mrs Ashton Cross already had a kennel of Bloodhounds and a famous Arab stud but, on seeing her first Pekingese while out walking in Piccadilly, decided this was the breed for her and her daughters. She began buying stock and, with her excellent eye, had soon started breeding under the prefix Alderbourne which was to become famous worldwide. She kept a kennel of over 200 dogs. According to visitors, they were kept in large groups with plenty of room to play and had their own obstacle course. They were also entered for obedience classes and, in fact, became so good that they made the bigger dogs look foolish.

Mrs Ashton Cross had four daughters who looked after the dogs with a string of kennel-girls. Marjorie and Cynthia carried on showing and breeding after the death of their mother, and I remember them in the ring always wearing white gloves so they did not put any of the grease from their hands on to the coats. Cynthia judged her last Championship show in 1977 but retained an interest in the breed until her death in the 1980s.

FAMOUS STUD DOGS

Other famous dogs of the period before the First World War were Ch. Broadoak

Ch. Toydom Manzee and his son, Ch. Toydom Manzee-Tu, pictured in the 1930s.

Beetle who was a black and tan, Sutherland Avenue Ouen Teu T'ang who was litter brother to Chu-Erh, both bred by Mrs Weaver. She never showed as she was frightened of the dogs getting distemper, which was a terrible killer in those days, so she sold stock to other kennels. Both of these dogs became famous stud forces and, although carrying the same pedigree, looked very different and produced individual-looking stock. Ch. Chinky Chog, who was actually bred in India from direct imports from China, became a very important outcross for the other strains.

TWO TYPES
Dog shows started up again in 1919 and the Alderbournes were the main force in the ring, followed closely by a name that is still known today, the Cavershams. Miss de Pledge based her kennel on the Alderbournes but, with careful outcrossing to the kennels of the time such as Sherhill, Remenham and Boltonia, she established a line on which a number of modern kennels have been based.

In the twenties and thirties, due to the difficulties of travel, there were two distinctive types of Pekes – the northern type which was larger, heavier and slightly coarse, and the southern type who was more compact and appeared more glamorous.

A dog who was the result of a mating between a northern dog, Boltonia Tai Choo, and a southern bitch, Ch. Sha-Sha of Caversham, really made the Cavershams famous. He was Tai Choo of Caversham who went on to sire many Champions both in Britain and in America. One of the most famous dogs of the twenties was Ch. Tai Yang of Newnham who won the CC at Crufts four times and ended his career with 43 CCs. He was also the first Peke to win BIS at a Championship show.

DESCRIPTIONS OF THE BREED

We have descriptions of the early show Pekes, sturdy and small with fiddle-shaped bodies, deep chests and narrow waists, broad fronts, short front legs well bowed, good manes and tails and long ear fringes, very dark eyes and noses quite pronounced. In size, they varied from 5-10 lbs. The modern Breed Standard was approved by the Kennel Club in 1950, but Pekingese have one of the earliest 'standards' in a poem written by the Dowager Empress T'sun Hsi.

"Let the Lion Dog be small, let it wear the swelling cape of dignity around its neck, let it display the billowing standard of pomp above its back.

Let its face be black, let its forefront be shaggy, let its forehead be straight and low. Let its eyes be large and luminous, let its ears be set like the sails of a war junk, let its nose be like that of the monkey god of the Hindus.

Let its forelegs be bent so that it shall not desire to wander far or leave the Imperial precincts. Let its body be shaped like that of a hunting lion spying for its prey.

Let its feet be tufted with plentiful hair that its footfall may be soundless and, for its standard of pomp, let it rival the whisk of the Tibetans yak which is flourished to protect the Imperial litter from flying insects.

Let it be lively that it may afford entertainment by its gambols, let it be timid that it may not involve itself in danger, let it be domestic in its habits that it may live in amity with the other beasts, fishes or birds that find

Ch. Toydom Ch'ien Men: The youngest Champion at the outbreak of the Second World war.

Ch. Toydom Ts'zee: Best of Breed Crufts 1956, winner of 18 CCs.

protection in the Imperial Palace and for its colour, let it be that of the lion – a golden sable to be carried in the sleeve of a yellow robe or the colour of a red bear or a black and white bear, or striped like a dragon, so that there may be dogs appropriate to every costume in the Imperial wardrobe.

Let it venerate its ancestors and deposit offerings in the canine cemetery of the Forbidden City on each new moon.

Let it comport itself with dignity, let it learn to bite the foreign devils instantly.

Let it be dainty in its food so that it shall be known as an Imperial dog by its fastidiousness, shark fins and curlew livers and the breasts of quails, on these may it be fed, and for drink give it the tea that is brewed from the spring buds of the shrub that groweth in the province of Hankow or the milk of the antelopes that pasture in the Imperial parks. Thus shall it preserve its integrity and self respect, and for the day of sickness let it be anointed with the clarified fat of the legs of a sacred leopard, and give it to drink a throstle's eggshell full of the juice of the custard app in which has been dissolved three pinches of shredded rhinoceros horn and apply it to piebald leeches.

So shall it remain – but if it die, remember *thou* too art mortal."

2 THE PEKINGESE PUPPY

The Pekingese has a unique charm, and, fortunately for us, the breed has undergone major improvements. You may have known a Peke some years ago, and your memory could well be of a snuffly, snappy little dog that seemed to spend most of its life being carried. Luckily, they are nothing like that now.

Today, the wonderful character of the Pekingese is fully in evidence. This small, impressive-looking dog is remarkably fearless, and this is combined with a most affectionate nature. Certainly they are no longer thought of as an old lady's dog or a lap dog. They like attention and cuddles – what dog does not? – but they also like doing their own thing. Contrary to popular belief, they enjoy going for walks, and, although they cannot move fast, they can cover quite a distance!

FINDING A BREEDER
This aristocratic breed should never be bought from an advertisement in a paper. If you know someone with a Peke, ask where they got it. Contact your national Kennel Club for lists of breeders, and for the name of a breed club secretary who will be able to advise.

When you get in touch with a breeder, do not expect that puppies will be available just like that – they are not items of merchandise that you buy off the shelf. Be prepared to undergo some pretty searching questions on why you want a Peke, and what your family circumstances are. A Peke and very young children do not really go together. A small, fluffy puppy looks too much like a toy, and it is very hard to explain to a child under five years old that you cannot pick it up by one leg or pull its ears.

Your home environment will also come under scrutiny. Is your garden properly fenced? Do you have a pond? Ponds are very dangerous for Pekingese

The charm of the Pekingese is second to none, but think carefully before taking on the responsibility of owning a puppy.

Photo: Keith Allison.

adults as well as puppies – if they fall in they can quickly get dragged down with the weight of their water-logged coats.

CHOOSING A PUPPY

If you meet a breeder's criteria, you will be invited to view the puppies. Take your family with you, but only those who are going to live with the dog – not your granny or the lady next door who just happens to fancy a drive out on a Sunday afternoon!

When you see the pups, watch them for a while before you ask permission to handle them. There is nothing worse than a stranger reaching out and grabbing little puppies. Remember you smell very different to the people they have been used to, and your size is daunting, so let them get used to you. There is nothing that annoys me more (and I am sure this applies to other breeders) than someone leaning over to pick up a puppy, while talking loudly, before the pup has had a chance to take in the new situation. It would not be surprising if even the boldest pup tried to run away.

Sit and watch the puppies while you talk to the breeder, and then you will be able to see how different they all are in personality. Just because they do not rush up to you to be picked up does not mean they are timid. Remember, they are Pekingese.

MALE OR FEMALE?

Now is the time to decide whether you want a male or a female. Most people arrive with firm ideas of what sex they want and leave with the opposite. There are slight drawbacks to both, although I feel the male has more advantages. House training is fairly easy with either sex, as the Peke is an intelligent dog who wants to please. If a male has been with you from puppyhood, there is no reason why he should lift his leg in the house or do embarrassing things with visitors' legs. Most of those things happen when a dog is living with an unneutered female who is coming into season.

Bitches come into season roughly every six months, and, as Pekes are such a small breed, there is not really much mess. Obviously, you must confine her to the garden during this period. If you intend to have your bitch spayed, it is advisable to wait until she has had her first season. After neutering, it is likely that she will grow much more coat, which will be of a fairly woolly texture.

In temperament there is very little difference. Males of smaller breeds, especially in the Toy Group, do not have the macho attack attitude of the bigger guarding breeds. Bitches can sometimes get a little temperamental when they are either in season or coming up to it.

COLOUR

Colour is a matter of personal choice. Most Pekes nowadays are shades of fawn from pale silver fawn through to fawn brindle which has black hairs mingled in. Reds are not as popular as they once were. This is because they do not carry as much coat, which is a disadvantage for a show dog.

For a pet, colour should be of least importance and unless you want a black Peke, which are usually only bred by specific breeders, then any litter you see will contain puppies with light-coloured fluffy coats – the main difference between them will be in the extent of their black facial markings. A full black face is not a prerequisite, and I think when the black colouring is confined to the muzzle, more of the expression coming from the eyes can be seen.

Ch. Delwin Another Ts 'zee:
A parti-coloured Pekingese.

Photo: Keith Allison.

Black is the preserve
of specialised breeders.

Photo: Keith Allison.

In fawn colours, the extent of black markings on the face will vary.   *Photos: Keith Allison.*

SHOW OR PET

If you are looking for a puppy to show, make sure you tell the breeder of your intention in the first place. There is nothing worse for a breeder than to see a dog that was sold as a pet turning up in the show ring. The reason that the puppy was sold as a pet was because it was not quite good enough for showing. The fault may be very small, but the breeder had decided that this particular dog would be better placed in a home as a companion. If a 'pet' is taken into the show ring, other exhibitors look at it and see the breeder's prefix and wonder why an inferior dog has been sold as a show prospect, not knowing the circumstances. Equally, it is very dispiriting to take a sub-standard dog into the ring and to keep on losing – it is enough to put you off showing, and the would-be breeder/exhibitor drops out of the dog scene. You might have longer to wait if you want a show prospect, but it will be worth it, especially when you win your first award.

When a breeder offers you a puppy for showing, there is no guarantee that it will turn out good enough, let alone whether it will win. The younger you buy your puppy, the more risk you run as to its development. You cannot be sure that its mouth will finish correctly when its second teeth come through, whether it will grow enough coat, whether it will be too big or too small.

It might go high on the leg, or its chest might not develop between its legs. There are so many things that can change during puppyhood that anyone who says they can pick out the good ones when they are just born is kidding themselves. If you buy a puppy at six months of age or older, then you must expect to pay more for it as the breeder has seen it through all its teething problems – which can change the look of the face from beautiful at six weeks to rather plain at six months. The opposite is also true, of course. If you can afford it, this is the best plan.

It is your decision whether to have a male or a female. I personally prefer males as I find them easier to show. They seem to want to please you more. They do not have off-days because of their hormones. They do not spend time out of the ring while they cast their coats, and they carry much more coat at the same time and look more dignified. It is the same in much of the animal world. The male always looks more glamorous. However, many people prefer to start with a bitch, as they have the option of breeding with her at a future date.

If you are offered a dog as a pet, do not think you are just getting the rubbish – far from it. Pekingese do not have many puppies in a litter – on average two to four – and most of them go to companion homes. Even if these dogs are a bit bigger than the Standard states, or have some other minor fault, I know they are going to be loved and spoilt; they will be allowed the freedom of the house, they will go out in the car for expeditions, and will probably go away with their family on holiday. Surely that is the life we want for all the puppies we bring into the world?

THE OLDER DOG

Sometimes if a puppy is not available, or your circumstances mean that a puppy would not be suitable, you may be offered an adult. Don't dismiss this without thinking about it. Usually breeders are willing to place adults in good homes for two main reasons. A bitch may have had a rough time giving birth – she may have had a caesarean, or she may have had problems rearing pups – and so the breeder does not want to put her through it again. A male may have been a show dog that had not quite made the grade at the junior stage – twelve to eighteen months. As males really only have one life as a show and stud, if they are not good enough to win at high level then nobody is going to want to use them at stud. In either of these cases, it is better that the dog or bitch has the rest of its long life in a loving family home rather than sitting in a kennel getting lower and lower down the pecking order.

Although these adults go to new homes with more of a memory of their previous routine, they soon settle when they realise they are getting their owner's undivided attention. I always let my young adults go on a month's trial, and if they do not settle they come back to me, and I try to find something else for the prospective owners. In thirty years of doing this, I have only had one dog returned, and that was the result of a marital break-up.

MAKING THE CHOICE

Let us assume you have now found a reputable breeder who has puppies available although not ready to leave home yet. You have been over and seen, not only the pups, but their mother and, if possible, their father – although he may well live elsewhere. You probably will have seen other members of the canine family, perhaps granny, cousins or an aunt.

The puppies should look fit and healthy with bright eyes and no discharge. They should smell nice, their ears should be clean, and their little tails should be well up over their backs, signalling they are happy and confident. After talking to the breeder about the reasons you want a Peke, discussing your home life, answering questions and listening to their opinions on individual pups, you make a choice. Most reputable breeders will not let their pups go until they have had at least the initial course of injections, so be patient if you have to wait. Do not expect to be able to buy a puppy at Christmas time, wait until afterwards – there is too much going on in a house at that time to be able to give enough

GROWTH AND DEVELOPMENT

Left: Six weeks old, resembling a small, fluffy toy.

Photo: Keith Allison.

Right: Twelve weeks old: Many breeders prefer to wait until this age before a puppy goes to his new home.

Photo: Keith Allison.

Left: Six months old: Ch. Guzmac's Dame's Solitaire, owned and bred by Mrs M. MacDonald. As the puppy gets older, it is easier to assess show potential.

Right: Fourteen months old: This youngster is just coming into his junior coat.

Photo: Keith Allison.

attention to a young puppy who needs regular meals of his own food, not rich Christmas fare. People will be too busy to take him out and so his toilet routine will be upset. Children should be old enough to be able to wait until after the excitement of the holiday season is over.

COST

Pekingese are relatively expensive compared to most other breeds. This is mainly because they do not have many in a litter and, if they are born by Caesarean, there has been quite a high vet's bill before the breeder has started feeding, worming or vaccinating them.

If you want a show dog, you must expect to pay more, as nobody is going to sell you a show prospect for the same price as a pet, especially if they are exhibitors themselves. Bitches are usually more expensive than dogs and harder to obtain. For some reason, everyone seems to want a bitch, even pet buyers. The older a show prospect is when sold, the more it will cost, as the breeder has taken the risks of it not finishing correctly and now it is ready to go in the ring.

COLLECTING YOUR PEKE

On collection day try not to go late in the day, especially if you have a long journey home. It can be very upsetting for a pup to leave his siblings and familiar surroundings and to go off in a strange car, with strange people, and then arrive at his new home at night-

To begin with, your Peke will miss the rivalry of his littermates at mealtimes, but he will soon make up for it!   Photo: Keith Allison.

time. Make sure you allow your pup a few hours of daylight to investigate your house and gardens before he is left alone.

The breeder will give you the puppy's pedigree and registration certificate or application with his official name, a vaccination certificate (if applicable), and details of when he has been wormed. He should also have a diet sheet and a small amount of his regular food to cover his first day in his new home in case you have not already got a supply in. Short-term insurance cover may also be provided.

The breeder will have demonstrated how to pick up a Pekingese correctly, with one hand supporting the weight of his chest and one hand under his rear end. *Never* pick a puppy up by his legs, and only in cases of real emergency, such as dogs fighting, would you hold him by the scruff of the neck. Keep the puppy close to your body so you can restrain him if he tries to jump down. When putting him down on the ground, always make sure all four legs are on the floor before letting go.

ARRIVING HOME

If your puppy has not had his full course of vaccinations, take him straight home and keep him in the confines of your garden and do not allow contact with other dogs. Even if the other dogs belonging to friends and family have been inoculated and are fit and healthy, they could have been in contact with a sick dog and be a carrier of a communicable disease.

When you first arrive home, carry the puppy out into the garden or wherever you want him to use as a toilet area, and let him sniff about for a bit. He will probably urinate after a little while and when he does praise him so he knows he is a good boy. If he does not want to go – and I do not intend you to stand outside in the freezing cold or pouring rain for hours – then take him in the kitchen or wherever there is a washable floor and put a couple of newspapers down near to the back door. Most puppies are paper-trained, but they are like human babies and need to 'go' often, so you will be picking up paper for a while, especially if your pup is only twelve weeks old when he comes to you.

Do not be cross if there are accidents in the house, just say "No", in a firm voice, and take him to the newspaper. Pekes are very intelligent and will soon learn. It is important they quickly get into a routine of being taken out first thing in the morning (and that is the minute you appear downstairs, not when you have had your first cup of coffee), after every meal, after a sleep, and last thing at night.

A puppy that is used to a crate will soon learn to regard it as his own special place.

A soft dog bed will also be appreciated.

Photo: Keith Allison.

THE FIRST FEW DAYS

If you have bought a travelling crate to bring your puppy home in, then let him use this as his bed, with a blanket, and leave the door open so he can get out for a drink and to go to the toilet. You will find he will go in it when he wants a sleep, or if he just wants some time to himself. All the family, especially children, should respect that this is his private place and he should not be disturbed. You can also buy puppy pens, which are panels of wire mesh, which you can extend as your puppy grows.

It is advisable to follow the breeder's diet sheet as this is what the puppy is used to, and the diet is based on the experience of someone who is used to rearing puppies. If you feel you must make a change, then do it gradually. A complete change will probably cause an upset stomach and diarrhoea, and put the puppy back in his toilet training. He might not eat as much as the breeder

has indicated because he has not got the competition from his brothers and sisters, but do not worry, once he has settled in he will clear his bowl at every meal. Pekes are the Labradors of the Toy dog world!

GROOMING

I start grooming at about six weeks with the puppy on my knee. Before that, I just make sure trousers are kept clean, usually by running lukewarm water from the tap over soiled back ends. This is much gentler than combing and dragging hair out.

It is only play-grooming to begin with, laying them on their backs so they get used to having their tummy area brushed, firstly with a bit of talcum powder sprinkled into the hair and brushed out with a soft brush. Then I turn them over and do the same on the main body and tail. A number of breeders stand puppies on the table and

25

start grooming properly at six weeks old, but I feel they are still babies and their coats should not need much attention at that age.

At about ten weeks they should be used to taking their worming tablet hidden in a small piece of best minced (chopped) beef and swallowing it without knowing they have had it. They should also be used to having their ears gently wiped out with cotton buds (cotton). There should be no need to be poking about with cotton buds in such young delicate ears as, if the dam had perfectly clean ears and no infections, they cannot have dirty ears. As they get older, some pups will seem to have more wax and, because of their heavy ear leathers, will tend to get more dirt lodging in the ear canal which, because the ear gets warm, will cause the dog to scratch and dislodge the dirty wax which will need cleaning out.

If a puppy is going to a pet home at 12 weeks of age, he should be used to standing on a worktop and being fully brushed with a nylon and bristle brush, and to having his ears wiped out (remember, never put water in the ear). There are a number of good ear cleaners you can buy at the pet shop, otherwise use baby oil on cotton wool. If the ears are really dirty, the vet will prescribe ear drops.

Get him used to having his face wiped and make sure his eyes are clean. One of the causes of eye ulcers is dogs rubbing their faces on the carpet or against a rough surface to try and get a hair off their eye and ending up with a sore eye or worse. You know how irritating it is when you get an eyelash in your eye, so imagine what it must be like when you cannot do anything about it. One of the main features of a Pekingese is their large, dark, lustrous eyes.

A Peke puppy coat will be mainly fluff until about four months of age when the longer junior coat will start appearing. This is when they need more regular grooming, certainly twice a week. Do not be too rough with the brush as you can do more harm than good, pulling out the coat which will take quite a while to grow back in.

I will go into more detail about grooming in the chapter about showing, but for a puppy you really only need a Mason Pearson nylon and bristle brush or similar and a good metal comb with fine and wide teeth (easier to use than the brush if your puppy has a knot). The secret is to sprinkle the knot with talcum powder to make it easier to gently separate the hair with your fingers before gently teasing with the comb. You notice I keep saying "gently" – that is the secret with Pekingese grooming. If you think to yourself "every hair I pull out will take at least six months to grow back", that should encourage you to go gently as your prospective show puppy could end up nearly bald in time for his first show.

The only part of a Peke coat that needs trimming is the hair under the feet and gently around the toe fringes. You are safer here with a pair of round-ended scissors because, if the puppy has tickly feet and wriggles, there is less chance of cutting his pads.

I am not a fan of bathing Pekes and there should be no reason why a puppy would need a bath. If, due to something he has eaten that has disagreed with him, he gets loose motions and badly soils his trousers, the easiest method is to stand him in the sink or shower tray and direct a lukewarm stream of water from a shower spray on to his trousers so that the dirt is washed straight off. Only if it was really smelly would I use a bit of shampoo afterwards.

EXERCISE

Do not be too keen to take your puppy for a walk. He will be getting quite enough exercise playing in the garden, especially if you are there with him playing games. Pekes are not the breed to play with a hard ball as they find it impossible to pick up but there are other toys they love. Soft toys or woolly balls can be held in the teeth and the

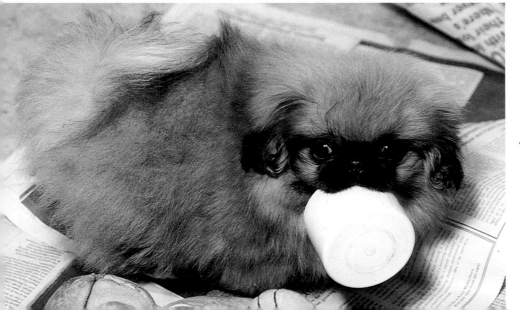

Peke puppies are very playful and games provide a useful means of exercise.

thing mine love most of all is the top of an aerosol can. Not only can they carry this by the rim but, when they drop it, it rolls and they can chase it.

LEAD TRAINING

You will very quickly have realised that Pekes can be very stubborn and if you have not, lead training will soon let you know! I find the easiest way to get puppies used to the lead is to put the collar on and just leave it on for a couple of days until they are used to the irritation around their neck, before attaching the lead.

I use the narrow nylon type which is not too heavy. You can keep adjusting the size as the puppy grows. When fastening a collar, always leave enough space to insert your thumb so that it is not too tight so as to choke, but not so loose that he can pull out of it. Initially, the puppy will scratch or rub his head against the furniture or along the carpet, trying to get it off. Take his mind off the collar by offering him a few tidbits of something special like cheese or chicken.

I always start lead training just before a puppy's mealtime. Attach the lead and gently start walking, calling his name and offering him a tidbit. I use cubes of cheese for this and, as the puppy is ready for food, this usually takes his mind off the fact that you have him attached to you and want him to go somewhere he might not.

When you first start lead training, it is easier just to do it for five minutes two or three times a day. The pup does not get bored and you do not get short-tempered when he digs his heels in and refuses to move. You will be surprised how strong a Peke puppy can be when he sits there trying to get his head out of the collar and flatly refuses to put one foot in front of the other.

This early training should be done in the confines of your own garden, mainly because your pup will probably not have finished his vaccinations yet, and so should not be out where other dogs have been. Also it can be very embarrassing when a little ball of fluff weighing no more than 5 lbs (2.25 kg) digs his heels in and refuses to move

Make sure your house and garden are puppy-proofed, as the inquisitive Peke will investigate anything that looks interesting.

under his own steam. Dragging him will not help!

Once puppies have had their vaccinations, then you should take them out, not only locally but in the car so they get used to it and are able to adapt to strange noises such as traffic and to meeting more people.

SOCIALISATION

Years ago, when you could take dogs into shops and everywhere else with you, they got used to noises and people very quickly. Now there are so many restrictions placed on dog owners, you have to work harder at socialising your puppy. Remember that wherever you go, you must always clean up after your puppy.

Puppies do not require a lot of lead walking; this is not a Golden Retriever that needs taking around the block three times a day. Just walk a couple of hundred yards initially to get the pup used to the noise of traffic will suffice. If he shrinks away at the noise of cars, do not be too quick to pick him up, bend down to him and reassure him that all is well, at the same time as stroking him. Be gentle with him at first and he will soon become more confident. Do not drag him along the pavement if he is obviously terrified of the big noisy world, as he will always remember these early excursions and if they start off badly then he will never enjoy going for walks.

When he is confident and enjoys going out with you then lengthen the distance but remember, this is never going to be a breed that wants or needs a five-mile hike!

LEAVING YOUR PUPPY

Pups should never be left longer than four hours as that is the limit that they can go between toilet visits, and I, personally, would not leave adults much longer than that. It is not fair to them if they are house-clean as they can make themselves ill by not being able to relieve themselves when necessary. There is no point being cross with a dog on your return if he has made any sort of mess. You can point at the offending thing and say "naughty boy" but never smack him. Your dog will not connect what he might have done hours ago with you telling him off now. He will only think you shout at him when you come home, which could worry him in the future.

CAR TRAVEL

If your puppy is going to be travelling with you in the car and certainly if he is going to shows, you should buy a travelling box. There are many different kinds on the market, some closed-in plastic with a front-opening mesh door and others all mesh with a lid or front-opening door. Do not get one too small as you will only have to buy another when your puppy has grown, so you might as well start with one that is going to last you.

29

A travelling crate is the safest way to transport your Pekingese. *Photo: Keith Allison.*

A comfortable size for an adult dog is 18 ins high x 16 ins wide (46 cms x 41 cms). Put comfortable bedding in the bottom when your puppy is younger so he will feel at home. You can also use this as his bed if you stay in an hotel or with a friend overnight. A show dog gets used to his crate and will run to it when you get it out the night before a show.

Do not take your puppy out in the car straight after a meal. He will vomit, always associate cars with being sick and dribble all the way there. If you are going to a show, the last thing you need is a soaking wet dog the moment you arrive. If you know you are going in the car, it is better for the puppy (or adult) to miss a meal and to be fed when you reach your destination.

A wire mesh crate is safer if you are going in the car when the sun is out, as you can open the windows and the air will blow through, keeping your dog cooler. Remember you should never leave a dog in the car if there is the slightest chance that the sun will shine on it. Cars, even with the windows ajar, can become like ovens and no dog can cope with that sort of heat, especially not Pekingese with their short nasal passages and big fur coats.

If you have to travel with your dog in the heat of the day, put a cold, wet towel over the top of the crate so that the moisture can drop on to the dog. A lot of exhibitors use ice packs under a layer of paper in the bottom of the box. This is fine if you have not got far to go and they will stay frozen for the length of your journey. One of the breed's successful exhibitors, who lives in Scotland and often has 800-mile round trips to shows, uses marble slabs (like those used for rolling out pastry) in the base of his crates. They stay cool all the time and the dogs are more comfortable on them than they would be on wet, thawing ice packs. The disadvantage is that they make the crates very heavy to pick up. But, if they help to alleviate the distress of an overheated dog, it is a small price to pay.

3 THE BREED STANDARD

Every breed has a Breed Standard. This is a blueprint for the breed – a description of the points that would be found in the ideal dog. Breeders are always trying to produce a dog that is as close to the Standard as possible.

I have reproduced here the British and American Standards and then discussed the British Standard, to fill in some of the points which go to make up this unique breed.

In my opinion, the Pekingese is the hardest breed of dog to judge and those that say otherwise perhaps do not understand what makes a correct Pekingese.

The Standard that the Kennel Club issues is based loosely on the description of the Ideal Palace Dog, "dropped from the lips of Her Imperial Majesty, T'su Hsi, the Dowager Empress" which closed Chapter One.

In the early days in the UK, the Standard included points. The head was given 35 points initially and coat only 15. What a turnaround there is now, as coat seems to be the most important thing to some breeders and exhibitors! The Standard also mentions soundness as essential three times, and this is very important in a breed which is built so differently from all others. The way an unsound Pekingese moves can often be thought correct by someone who does not understand the format of the front assembly in relation to the hindquarters.

The Standards are the blueprint that we should all strive to breed for and judge against. To get it exactly right is to have a perfect Peke and that is what we should all be striving for. Do not accept second best either in breeding, showing or judging – especially in judging, because, if incorrect specimens are given top awards, then they will be used in breeding and the breed will go downhill.

The good of the breed is in judges' hands – sometimes more than in

Ch. Shiarita Diamond Lil: Winner of 20 CCs.   *Photo: Diane Pearce.*

breeders. Judge to the Standard and do not let fashion, fads or friends influence your judgement.

THE KENNEL CLUB STANDARD

GENERAL APPEARANCE: Small, well balanced, thick-set dog of dignity and quality.

CHARACTERISTICS: Leonine in appearance with alert and intelligent expression.

TEMPERAMENT: Fearless, loyal, aloof but not timid or aggressive.

HEAD AND SKULL: Head large, proportionately wider than deep.

EYES: Large, clear, round, dark and lustrous.

EARS: Heart-shaped, set level with the skull and carried close to the head, with long profuse feathering. Leathers not to come below line of muzzle.

MOUTH: Level lips, must not show teeth or tongue. Firm under-jaw essential.

NECK: Very short and thick.

FOREQUARTERS: Short, thick, heavily boned forelegs; bones of forelegs slightly bowed, firm at shoulder. Soundness essential.

BODY: Short, broad chest and good spring of ribs, well slung between forelegs with distinct waist, level back.

HINDQUARTERS: Hindlegs lighter than forelegs but firm and well shaped. Close behind but not cow-hocked: Soundness essential.

Skull broad, wide and flat between ears; not domed; wide between eyes. Nose short and broad, nostrils large, open and black; muzzle wide, well wrinkled with firm under-jaw. Profile flat with nose well set between eyes. Pronounced stop. Black pigment essential on nose, lips and eye rims.

FEET: Large and flat, not round. Standing well up on feet, not on pasterns. Front feet slightly turned out.

TAIL: Set high, carried tightly, slightly curved over back to either side. Long feathering.

GAIT/MOVEMENT: Slow dignified rolling gait in front. Typical movement not to be confused with a roll caused by slackness of shoulders. Close action behind. Absolute soundness essential.

COAT: Long, straight with profuse mane extending beyond shoulders forming a cape round neck; top coat coarse with thick undercoat. Profuse feathering on ears, back of legs, tail and toes.

COLOUR: All colours and markings are permissible and of equal merit, except albino or liver. Parti-colours evenly broken.

SIZE: Ideal weight not exceeding 5 kgs (11 lbs) for dogs and 5.5 kgs (12 lbs) for bitches. Dogs should look small but be surprisingly heavy when picked up; heavy bone and a sturdy well-built body are essentials of the breed.

FAULTS: Any departure from the foregoing points should be considered a fault and the seriousness with which the fault should be regarded should be in exact proportion to its degree.
NOTE Male animals should have two apparently normal testicles fully descended into the scrotum.

© *The Kennel Club 1994*

THE AMERICAN BREED STANDARD

The Board of Directors of the American Kennel Club has approved the following revised Standard for the Pekingese as submitted by the Pekingese Club of America, Inc.

GENERAL APPEARANCE
The Pekingese is a well-balanced, compact dog with heavy front and lighter hindquarters. It must suggest its Chinese origin in it directness, independence, individuality and expression. Its image is lion-like. It should imply courage, boldness and self-esteem rather than prettiness, daintiness or delicacy.

SIZE, SUBSTANCE, PROPORTION
Size/Substance – The Pekingese should be surprisingly heavy when lifted. It has a stocky, muscular body. The bone of the forequarters must be very heavy in relation to the size of the dog. All weights are correct within the limit of 14 pounds, provided that type and points are not sacrificed.
Disqualification : weight over 14 pounds.
Proportion – The length of the body, from the front of the breastbone in a straight line to the buttocks, is slightly greater than the height at the withers. Overall balance is of utmost importance.

Am. Ch. Pequest Picasso: Top Pekingese 1997, twice BIS Pekingese Club of America.

Photo: Jordan.

HEAD

Skull – The topskull is massive, broad and flat (not dome-shaped). The topskull, the high, wide cheekbones, broad lower jaw and wide chin are the structural formation of the correctly shaped face. When viewed frontally, the skull is wider than deep and contributes to the rectangular envelope-shaped appearance of the head. In profile, the Pekingese face must be flat. The chin, nose leather and brow all lie in one plane. In the natural position of the head, this plane appears vertical but slants very slightly backward from chin to forehead.

Nose – It is black, broad, very short and, in profile, contributes to the flat appearance of the face. Nostrils are open. The nose is positioned between the eyes so that a line drawn horizontally across the top of the nose intersects the center of the eyes.

Eyes – They are large, very dark, round, lustrous and set wide apart. The look is bold, not bulging. The eye rims are black and the white of the eye does not show when the dog is looking straight ahead.

Wrinkle – It effectively separates the upper and lower areas of the face.

The appearance is of a hair-covered fold of skin, extending from one cheek, over the bridge of the nose in a wide inverted V, to the other cheek. It is NEVER so prominent or heavy as to crowd the facial features nor to obscure a large portion of the eyes or the nose from view.

Stop – It is deep. The bridge of the nose is completely obscured from view by hair and/or the over-nose wrinkle.

Muzzle – This is very short and broad with high, wide cheekbones. The color of the skin is black. Whiskers add to the Oriental expression.

Mouth – The lower jaw is slightly undershot. The lips meet on a level plane and neither teeth nor tongue show when the mouth is closed. The lower jaw is strong, wide, firm and straight across at the chin. An excessively strong chin is as undesirable as a weak one.

Ears – They are heart-shaped and set on the front corners of the skull extending the line of the topskull. Correctly placed ears frame the sides of the face and with their heavy feathering create an illusion of additional width of the head.

Pigment – The skin of the nose, lips and eye rims is black on all colors.

NECK, BODY, TAIL

Neck – It is very short, thick and set back into the shoulder.

Body – This is pear-shaped and compact. It is heavy in front with well-sprung ribs slung between the forelegs. The broad chest, with little or no protruding breastbone, tapers to lighter lines with a distinct waist. The topline is level.

Tail – The base is set high; the remainder is carried well over the center of the back. Long, profuse straight feathering may fall to either side.

FOREQUARTERS

They are short, thick and heavy-boned. The bones of the forelegs are slightly bowed between the pastern and elbow. Shoulders are gently laid back and fit smoothly into the body. The elbows are always close to the body. Front feet are large, flat and turned slightly out. The dog must stand well up on its feet.

HINDQUARTERS

They are lighter in bone than the forequarters. There is moderate angulation and definition of stifle and hock. When viewed from behind, the rear legs are reasonably close and parallel and the feet point straight ahead.

Soundness is essential in both forequarters and hindquarters.

COAT

Body Coat – It is full-bodied, with a long, coarse textured, straight, stand-off coat and thick, softer undercoat.

The coat forms a noticeable mane on the neck and shoulder area with the coat on the remainder of the body somewhat shorter in length. A long and profuse coat is desirable providing that it does not obscure the shapeliness of the body, nor sacrifice the correct coat texture.

Feathering – Long feathering is found on the back of the thighs and forelegs, and on the ears, tail and toes. The feathering is left on the toes but should not be so long as to prevent free movement.

COLOR
All coat colors and markings, including parti-colors, are allowable and of equal merit.

GAIT
The gait is unhurried and dignified, with a slight roll over the shoulders. The rolling gait is caused by the bowed front legs and heavier, wider forequarters pivoting on the tapered waist and the lighter, straight parallel hindquarters. The rolling motion is smooth and effortless and is as free as possible from bouncing, prancing or jarring.

TEMPERAMENT: A combination of regal dignity, self-importance, self-confidence and exasperating stubbornness make for a good natured, lively and affectionate companion to those who have earned its respect.

The foregoing is a description of the ideal Pekingese. Any deviation should be penalized in direct proportion to the extent of that deviation.

FAULTS TO BE NOTED
- Dudley, liver or gray nose
- Light brown, yellow or blue eyes
- Protruding tongue or teeth
- Overshot upper jaw
- Wry mouth
- Ears set much too high, low or far back
- Roach or swayback
- Straight-boned forelegs

POINTS

Expression	5
Nose	5
Stop	5
Muzzle	5
Legs and feet	15
Tail	5
Skull	10
Eyes	5
Ears	5
Shape of body	20
Coat, feather & condition	10
Action	10
Total	100

Disqualification: weight over 14 pounds.

Approved : June 13, 1995
Effective: July 31, 1995

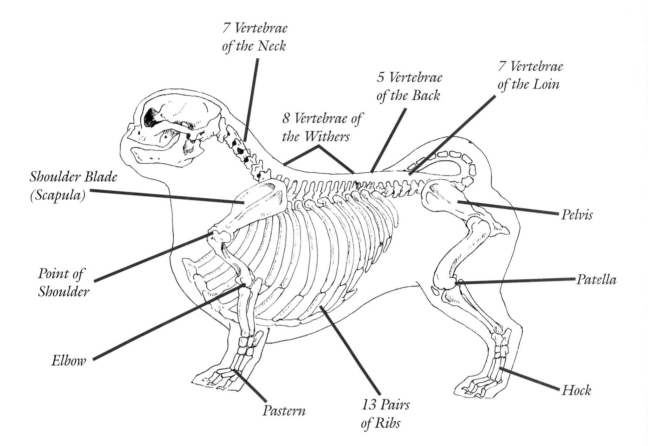

7 Vertebrae
of the Neck

5 Vertebrae
of the Back

7 Vertebrae
of the Loin

8 Vertebrae of
the Withers

Shoulder Blade
(Scapula)

Pelvis

Point of
Shoulder

Patella

Elbow

Hock

Pastern

13 Pairs
of Ribs

EXPLANATION AND ANALYSIS

GENERAL APPEARANCE

A Pekingese should present the appearance of a square dog. Viewed from the front, the topline is straight across and very wide, with a wide chest and width between the front legs. From the side view, he is low to ground, with a deep brisket, waisted topline and flat back line.

The Pekinese should be small but look very heavy. You should be surprised how heavy the dog is when you pick him up.

CHARACTERISTICS

This is what attracts you to the breed; its confidence and courage without aggression, its independence and aloofness without any signs of being timid or shy. We are attracted to the breed initially by what we hear about its independence and intelligence, not its

Correct outline.

Incorrect: Over-wrinkled.

Incorrect: Domed skull.

size or shape. I think most of us like the fact that Pekingese are so plucky and will stand up to anything, however large. This is only if they feel like it, because one of their main traits is stubbornness. They will usually only do something if they want to, but you feel they would support you to their last breath.

HEAD AND SKULL

The Pekingese is often described as a head breed which, to my mind, places far too much importance on the head and too little on the body and movement (although a good body and correct movement without a good head will mean that the dog is only average, and that is the last thing you should aim for).

Years ago the Standard used to say "head massive". This was removed as it was felt that breeding extra-large heads caused problems in whelping. Speaking

personally, I have not experienced any more difficulties in that area over the years, but I do feel we have lost something of the look of the breed as some heads are now positively small.

"Proportionally wider than deep" used to be described as "envelope-shaped". We should try to remember this as there are so many square faces in the breed, which not only have the wrong expression, but also tend to look common and that is one thing this quality oriental should never be. The forehead should be shallow and the top of the head between the ears should be absolutely flat. No suggestion of a rise or dome should be present.

There should be plenty of width between the ears, which should frame the face. There should also be plenty of width between the eyes, otherwise the face looks crowded. The nose should be well up between the eyes, so much so that an imaginary line could be drawn across the top of the nose which should go across the middle of the eyes.

The nostrils should be as large and open as possible. The nose should never be covered in any way by the wrinkle and the nostrils should never be pinched, which is not only ugly but very unhealthy as it affects breathing. Nor should there be a visible bridge on the nose; it should actually be tilted slightly backwards.

There should be as much width in the jaw as there is between the eyes, never any suggestion of a heart-shaped face or narrowness in the jaw. The wide, slightly undershot lower jaw is what gives the face its aristocratic expression as though it was looking down on everything.

The muzzle on either side of the mouth should be well cushioned and there should also be a chin. Absence of chin or a very weak chin results in a frog-like expression where the top lips hang loosely over the bottom ones instead of meeting.

The Standard only says black pigmentation essential on nose, lips and eye rims. A black face or muzzle is not a prerequisite, just a fashion which seems to have taken over. A Peke can have a self-coloured face and still have excellent pigment. Pigment is in the skin, not the coat.

EYES
The large eye is one of the main points of the breed that we are losing. Years ago, nearly every dog had large eyes and those that did not possess this lovely feature stood out because it made their expression look mean.

There should never be any trace of white as in a bolting, protruding eye and it should be as dark as possible. Some dogs still carry those lovely dark lines from the corner of the eyes towards the ears and the shadowy look of spectacles around the eyes, which adds to the expression of the face.

The eyes should be the first thing you see in a Peke's face and you should be drawn to those large dark pools and melt.

EARS
The ears must be set on the extreme ends of the skull to be correct. Too high up and in towards the middle of the skull gives a narrow, small head. Too far back and they fly back, especially when the dog starts moving, giving a very startled expression. When ears are set down too low towards the side of the head they will make the head look rounded.

The leathers of the ears themselves should never be long, but the fringes can be as long as they will grow. Although the Standard says "heart shaped" I doubt whether many people feel for this even on their own dogs – let alone when judging others.

MOUTH
One of the reasons why so many judges

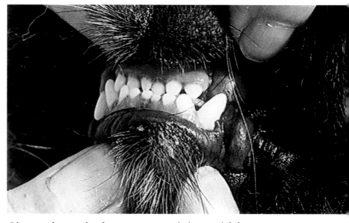

Six teeth on the bottom row giving width to the jaw. Correct bite, reverse scissor.
Photo: Keith Allison.

never open a Pekingese mouth, certainly in this country, is that there is nothing in the Standard that says anything about dentition or bite.

We know that to get width of jaw the ideal would be six teeth in a straight line along the bottom. To get the slight strength of bottom jaw, it is better if the mouth is slightly undershot (that is, the bottom teeth slightly more forward than the top teeth).

When judging, all you are asked to look for is that the dog neither shows teeth nor tongue. What is actually going on in the mouth is one of life's mysteries.

If the lips are not level, then the mouth could be wry, i.e. the lower jaw is at a different angle to the upper jaw, so the distance between the upper and lower teeth at one side of the mouth is not the same as at the other side. This is a serious fault and should be penalised.

NECK

For many years there was nothing in the Standard about the neck as it was so short as not to be worth mentioning.

There are now too many dogs with enough length of neck to lift their heads up and gaze at the sky!

A correctly constructed dog with a very short thick neck could not do this without causing himself great pain, or even falling over.

FOREQUARTERS

The legs must be short, as this is a dog that is low to the ground. Long legs not only alter the appearance but would also alter the movement. Because the body is heavy, and much heavier in front, the front legs must have heavy bone to support it.

The Pekingese is, in my opinion, the most difficult breed to judge because of its front assembly. Until you have put your hands on a correct front, you will never understand what a bowed front means or how it moves in that unique way.

The forechest should stand out in front of the dog, and the width of chest should be slung in between the legs.

The shoulders should fit tightly on to the ribcage and the bow comes from the shoulder to the elbow. The bow tends to accommodate the ribcage before straightening out to the ankle.

The neck is very short, no longer than two fingers' width. *Photo: Keith Allison.*

Correct width and depth of chest, and correct placement of front feet. Photo: Keith Allison.

Correct front.   *Incorrect: Out at elbow.*   *Incorrect: Straight-legged.*

A dog with a straight front would never have its ribcage well slung, as there would not be the room to accommodate it.

The curve between shoulder and elbow comes from the inside, i.e.

nearest to the chest, and not so that the elbow sticks out in a curve; that is unsoundness.

A lack of depth of chest is felt by putting a hand flat on the table and seeing how far it goes upwards before

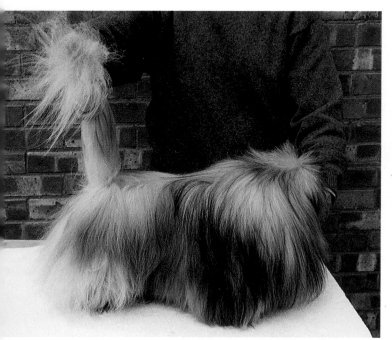

The back should be level, measured from the shoulders to the root of tail.

Photo: Keith Allison.

touching the bones of the chest, not the hair. If you are above elbow level, then the chest has no depth and the Peke will usually have straight legs.

BODY
The body should narrow down backwards like a pear, with the bones and substance getting lighter. A correctly built dog will appear front-heavy and, in fact, would topple forwards if picked up under the middle with one hand and not supported.

The back should be level from the base of the neck to the root of the tail. The back should not be too long, i.e. in loin, that is from end of ribs to tail, nor should it be too short in this area, as this will cause the dog to move rather like a Pomeranian.

The body should be very solid and substantial, which should come from the heavy bone – not from a fat stomach.

HINDQUARTERS
All of the hindquarters are lighter and finer than the front, but this does not mean spindly back legs.

The back legs are much closer together than the front, but not so close as to touch, and, when seen from the rear they should be straight and parallel. From the side you should be able to see the angle of the hock.

FEET
The feet should be large, never small and cat-like, and Pekes should stand just on their pads not further back on their pasterns.

Correct placement of hindlegs, not too close together or too far apart.

Photo: Keith Allison.

Correct rear.

Incorrect: Cow-hocks.

Incorrect: Weak, turned-out hocks.

The front feet should turn slightly outwards, when viewed from above, in a '10 to 2' position. They should never turn inwards, and, on a correct front, they should always move forward with plenty of width in between – otherwise the chest will be too narrow. They must be strong as they have a heavy body to support.

The back feet face forwards and walk in a straight line to offset the roll from the front.

TAIL
The tail must be set high on the end of the spine and be carried over the back, not up in the air or at half-mast. It should fall to either side, although

nowadays most people groom the tail to spread out like a fan over all the back.

A tail that is set too low will give the impression of more length of back and is usually indicative of incorrect hindquarter assembly.

It should be well feathered, and in the past it was said that the hair of the tail should reach the nape of the neck.

The tail should always be carried proudly over the back as a sign that the dog is not frightened or timid. A Pekingese with his tail down trailing behind him, is a sad, pitiful thing.

GAIT/MOVEMENT

The first word and the most important is "slow". You can only assess correct movement when the dog is walking slowly. If he moves correctly at a slow speed, you can be nearly certain before you handle him that he is constructed correctly. A dog that can stride out quickly is usually straight in front and probably has no width of chest.

A correct Pekingese movement is described as "rolling". This is due to the dog's body being heavy in the front and light behind so that his centre of gravity comes much nearer the head than in a normally proportioned dog. At the same time the fact that the hindlegs are close together and the forelegs wide apart imparts at each step a rolling movement towards the unsupported side.

A properly constructed Peke can never be walked very quickly before he would

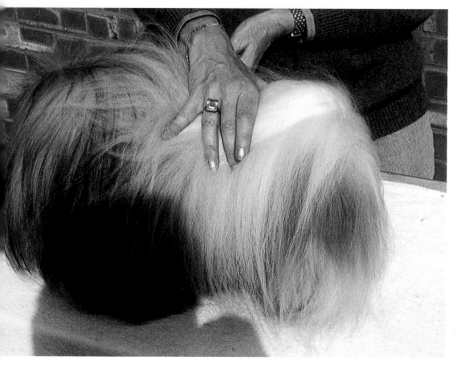

The correct high-set tail with long feathering.

Am. Ch. Morningstar Fascination: The coat is a great feature of the breed.

have to break into a run, usually moving both hindlegs together like a rabbit to stop himself toppling over sideways.

A Pekingese should move with dignity, not be rushing along like a terrier.

COAT

Due to exhibitors wanting more and more coat, even though the Standard mentions the word "profuse" in relation to the mane, the look of the Peke has changed dramatically over the years.

People who have not seen the breed for the last twenty years would hardly recognise it as the same. Now the coat is all over the body in great thickness and length, so there is no way to see the shape of the body.

Not only is there too much coat, but, to my mind, the worst thing is that it is totally the wrong texture. The top coat, especially on the mane, should be coarse, not soft and woolly. The coarse texture on the mane causes it to stand off from the body which, if correct, it should do without any help from lotions and sprays. Too many dogs now have manes which merge into their body coats and make them look shapeless.

The undercoat is softer and thick and it is this coat which stands slightly off from the body, covered by a long, straight top coat. It should not be thick around the loins or flanks or you will lose shape.

The only parts where the coat should be long are the ear fringes, backs of the

A full black mask: This is not a requirement of the Standard.

A pale fawn Pekingese with a black muzzle. The eyes are more expressive without the full black mask.

legs (more so on the front than the back), the tail, and the trousers or skirts, depending on the sex. Even these should only reach floor level as trailing skirts simply make a dog look longer.

One part of the coat over which present-day breeders have gone completely the opposite way is the hair on the feet. When I first came into the breed, the toe fringes, especially at the front, were very long. I felt they hampered the dogs' movement and looked untidy. Over the years, these have now become so trimmed they resemble those of a flat-footed cat.

COLOUR

All colours are allowed except liver and albino but, over the years, we have lost the deep reds, mainly because they did not carry the thick undercoats and so looked out of coat against their fawn and grey companions who did more winning because of this and were therefore used more at stud until the reds were bred out.

It was believed that, in the palaces in China, eunuchs would breed dogs to suit the colours of their master's robes. Certainly in the early days of the breed in England there was much more variation in colours, ranging from white and cream through fawn and white and grey and white parti-colours to fawns, reds, greys, brindles, blacks, and black and tans.

Due to two prepotent stud dogs being used in the last twenty years, most of the dogs in the ring in the UK are now fawn or a variation of it. These seem to be preferred sometimes over better dogs or not so glamorous a colour – especially when the fawns have black masks, which is something not asked for in the Standard.

If given the choice of two dogs of equal merit, I would select the one with the muzzle not the mask, as I feel you can see the expression and the eyes so much better when the black does not extend above the eyes.

Do remember an old saying: 'A good dog can never be a bad colour'.

SIZE
This is a very contentious topic in the breed as the size of the dogs and bitches has increased, certainly over the last fifteen years.

The dog should look small but substantial. There should be no signs of weediness. You may be surprised at how much a Pekingese weighs for its size. A big dog could well weigh 15 or 16 lb; that is what some must weigh now.

I think the American idea of being able to disqualify a dog over 14 lbs is excellent, as it must help to keep the size within the correct range.

My ideal weight for a male is 9 to 10 lbs. Although a bitch can be 1 lb heavier, this does not mean that she should be considerably bigger. Some people think that a brood bitch should have more length in back in order to produce pups easily but, in my opinion, bitches of the correct size and length are usually the easiest whelpers.

A number of exhibitors think they will win more with a larger dog covered in a mass of hair. They probably will – under judges who are as ignorant as they of the correct size for a Peke. However, the first word of the Standard is "small" and we must never forget that.

4 *IN THE SHOW RING*

This chapter is mainly aimed at the novice exhibitor as certainly, nowadays, most people who are showing their second or third dog will be giving everyone else advice. They will probably only have been showing two or three years but will be passing opinions on other people's dogs (mainly their faults, never their virtues), even though they have never handled them. They will be of the opinion that the reason they do not win very much is because they are not in with the right crowd or they are not judging – never that their dogs are not good enough.

But for those who have taken their time looking at Pekingese, talking to breeders and exhibitors and sitting at ringsides watching classes being judged and noting the breeding of dogs that they particularly like, even if they did not always win, this chapter will be of some help.

PREPARING TO SHOW

There are very few people who start off with their first puppy going to shows and winning a lot. This is not because the puppy is not good enough to win, but because you and he are novices and learning all the time – about grooming and presentation, about which classes to go for and which shows to enter.

Do not get disheartened if you fail to win or even get placed at the first few shows. You did not get behind the wheel of a car and expect to pass your driving test after the first few lessons, and this is very similar.

I am assuming that your puppy was fully inoculated when you bought him from the breeder and that his vaccination certificate was included in the paperwork, together with the registration certificate from your national kennel club and a diet sheet, which in the main, you are sticking to. Reputable breeders know what amounts of food your puppy needs; they have

Ch. Micklee Roc's Ruago: Winner of 26 CCs and Reserve BIS Crufts 1985.
The rewards of showing are great, but it takes hard work and dedication to reach the top.

probably been doing this for a few years and, even if you are going to make any changes to the actual format of the diet, you must do it gradually otherwise you are going to have upset tummies and a puppy probably not putting on the weight he should. Even a puppy should pick up 'heavy' and have the makings of solid bone.

Also, you will have a pedigree certificate which, initially, will just be a lot of strange names, but, as you progress in the show world, these names will become synonymous with certain people. Years ago, spectators were able to stand on a ringside and pick out the dogs that had connections with certain kennels by certain aspects of their looks. Nowadays that is not so

easy, as so many breeders switch from line to line – but it is still possible.

RING TRAINING

Before you take your puppy out into the show world you should have done some ring training with him so you both know what you are doing.

Your national kennel club can advise you on ring training classes in your area. As these are usually held at night, you want to be fairly local. Sometimes they are advertised in the veterinary surgery or a local pet shop, and if you bought your puppy locally, the breeder will know where they are held. Do also ask show people in your area, as not all ring training classes are suitable for Pekes. The ideal class is one catering just for Toy dogs but these are rare, so try and find one that is not full of exuberant Dobermans, Labradors and the other big breeds. These can often put a small dog off altogether.

For your first visit to the class, take your puppy in his travelling crate so he will feel secure and, as this is how he will be travelling to shows, it gets him used to car journeys. I also include his favourite toy in the crate as, sometimes, that is all that puppies will walk for when they feel unsure. Do not be in too much of a hurry to put him on the floor. The first night I usually just sit with them on my knee with their collar and lead attached and let people come up and talk to them. I let them get used to the noise of dogs barking, people talking and the other noises that happen in show halls which you can never create at home.

When you do put him on the floor to take part in a class, be very patient with him, talk to him a lot, show him the tidbits of cheese or whatever he really likes, and keep your eyes on the other dogs to see that none get too close and upset him.

A puppy upset in the early days of ring training may need a lot of time and patience to get his confidence back.

The classes are run in small halls and, as they are very popular, they usually get very busy, so it is better to get there at the start so your puppy can walk up and down before it gets packed with wall-to-wall dogs and people.

The purpose of the exercise is to recreate the show ring so the dogs are handled on the table and walked up and down just as they would be at a real show.

ON THE TABLE

When you put your puppy on the table for examination, if you have been practising at home, he should stand solidly with his tail up over his back. Always keep your hand on him to start with, as the last thing you want is for him to be so enthusiastic when the judge comes to examine him that he tries to jump off the table into their arms! Or the opposite, that he is so wary he backs off and falls off the edge. He will feel more confident with your hand gently stroking his tail over his back.

Do also ensure that the judge does not start trying to open his mouth to check bite. Be firm about this, as it will not happen in a real dog show unless the judge is ignorant of the Pekingese Breed Standard!

When a judge picks up your Pekingese to check that he is surprisingly heavy for his size, do ensure that he is held correctly. There is no need for him to be picked up in the air and turned to face the judge. A few inches off the table is all that is necessary to feel the weight. A quiet word later to the trainer should ensure that your puppy is not put off by this undignified flight into the air.

MOVING

You will be advised to walk with the puppy on your left side, so make sure your lead is fastened on the right side of his neck just under his ear.

If your puppy needs encouragement, show him the cheese, talk to him using his name, and lean down to him so you

The Pekingese must be trained to move correctly in the show ring. The dog should be on your left side, with the lead on the right side of the dog's neck, placed under the right ear. Photo: Keith Allison.

are in close contact. If he is very enthusiastic and gallops away, do not restrain him too much at first. It is better to have a puppy that you have to catch up with than one who will not put one foot in front of the other. In time, you can alter your pace to go with his slow dignified walk.

Get him used to the command "Stand" as you will be using it a lot to start with, especially on the table while he is being examined. Speaking as a judge, there is nothing more annoying than trying to assess a dog on the table that is trying to leap off, or turn round and climb up his owner's chest and for the owner just to stand there and say "He's such a handful". By the time your puppy gets to the show he should not be such a handful if he has had some training.

Pekes are judged quite a lot on the table, both individually and together with the rest of the class, so standing still will not only give the judge a better appreciation of how good a puppy is, but also will not annoy your fellow exhibitors whose own puppies are behaving themselves.

Peke puppies are just as naughty and mischievous as puppies of any other breed. As they mature they become more dignified and aloof, but you do not want them to be like robots. They should still have personality, so do not be too hard and firm in their puppy training. Remember to be lavish with praise when they get it right.

Grooming kit for a Pekingese.   *Photo: Keith Allison.*

I have said over the years to my dogs: "I will look after you, feed you, groom you and love you all your life. All I ask is two minutes of good showmanship in the ring." I recommend that other exhibitors should adopt the same approach.

SHOW GROOMING
Your puppy should have been groomed regularly before ever being entered for a show, but, as the big day draws near, he needs a bit of extra attention to detail.

Check that his pads are trimmed with round-ended scissors so not only are they clean but comfortable to walk on.

A cushion of hair under his feet can cause the soundest dog to walk badly. Cut nails a few days before the show then, if you make a mistake and cut the quick, it will have healed over and the dog will have forgotten about it. There is a number of different types of nail-clippers on the market and it is a matter of personal preference as to which one you use.

THE FEET
Although it says "profuse feathering on toes" in the Standard, I think all exhibitors trim to some degree. Really long fringes can look untidy and

ROUTINE CARE
Photos: Keith Allison.

Early training will ensure that your Pekingese is happy to stand on a table for grooming.

Trim under the pads with round-ended scissors.

Use nail-clippers to trim the nails, taking care not to cut into the quick.

The underside of the foot with the hair and the nail trimmed.

hamper a dog's movement. Do not trim them to look like a cat's feet; leave enough fringing to cover their nails. I do this by holding paws at the wrist and trimming around the shape of the foot, then putting the foot on the table to see how tidy it is before going back and having another gentle trim. Trim the front feet first as they are the ones most on view.

When doing the back feet, you will probably want to trim part way up the hock as well, as Pekes can grow quite thick tufts of hair there. Again, do a little to start with, as you can always go back later and tidy it up.

Lay the dog on his back and, if he is a male, make sure his sheath is clean. If needed, wash with cotton wool (cotton) and warm water. If he should be sore for any reason, gently apply ointment with a very clean finger or applicator.

As exhibitors cannot use talcum powder at UK shows nowadays, due to so many venues being withdrawn because of the amount of powder left behind on the floors, whatever you use the night before a show must be well brushed out. Not only does talcum powder help in cleaning the coat and making it easier to separate any knots, it also makes Pekes smell nicer. This practice will also work for any Peke exhibitor, regardless of nationality.

BATHING

Some people bath their show dogs, obviously not for every show, but probably a couple of times in a busy show season. If a dog is casting, this will get rid of any dead hair that is resisting coming out with the brush and can make the coat look more alive and healthy. Light fawn and red dogs look better after a bath as newsprint from their bedding, grooming sprays and general dirt certainly make their coat look dull.

Stand them in the kitchen sink or the shower and wet the coat thoroughly. It helps to stop water going in the ears if you plug them with cotton wool (cotton).

There are plenty of dog shampoos on the market. Do not be tempted to use one for human hair, as the pH balance is quite different. Massage well into the coat taking care not to get foam on to the face or near the eyes. Rinse thoroughly. As long as you are not shampooing too often, I see no reason to use conditioner.

Towel dry but do not rub too vigorously as this can cause mats. Just pat dry at the same time as having a warm air heater or hair dryer gently blowing on the coat to speed things up. When it is nearly dry start gently brushing, but do not do this when the coat is wet as you will drag the hair and damage it. Also never use a wire brush, always one with natural bristles and nylon.

Do make sure your dog is fully dry before letting him outside. Pekes are very hardy but lying about, perhaps on a concrete floor, with a damp chest will not do a dog any good.

BATHING
Photos: Keith Allison.

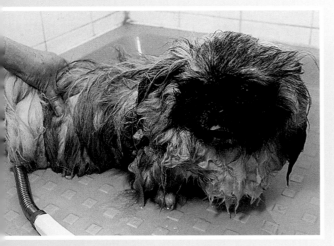

The coat must be soaked thoroughly.

Apply shampoo and work into a rich lather.

Rinse the shampoo out of the coat.

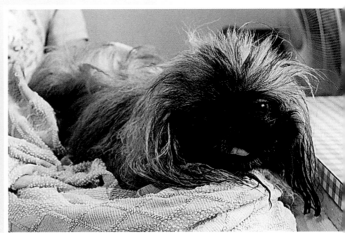

After bathing, remove the excess moisture with a towel.

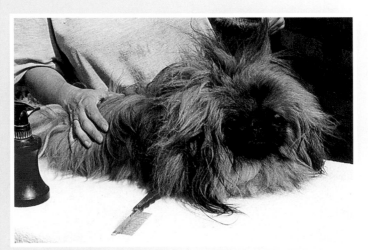

The coat should be brushed through.

BRUSHING
Photos: Keith Allison.

1. The well-trained Peke will be quite happy to lie on the grooming table. First, spray the coat before applying powder.

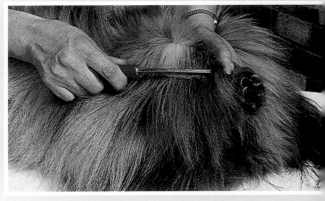

2. Comb the coat in layers, starting with the hair nearest the stomach.

3. Brush the coat from the root of the tail up to the head, then brush it back the correct way.

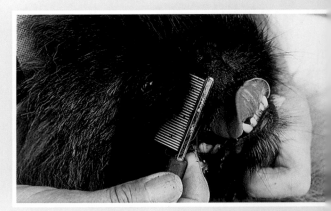

4. Take great care when combing the facial hair.

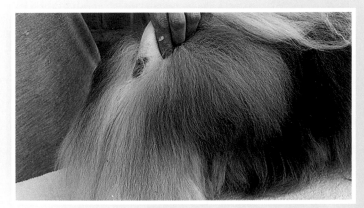

5. The tail is groomed last. It is brushed in sections down to the root.

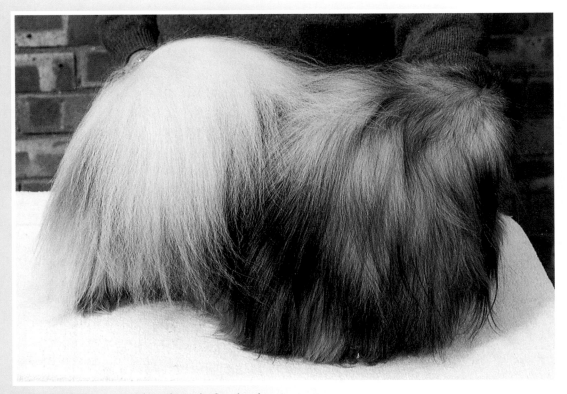

6. Beautifully groomed and ready for the show!

BRUSHING

Spray the coat first before powdering and brushing as this prevents the hairs breaking and splitting. There are so many canine coat sprays on the market now to choose from. Do not get anything with oil in it, as a greasy coat is the last thing you want. As a Peke coat should be coarse, look for a preparation made specifically for harsh or coarse coats.

Spray a small amount on the stomach and chest and head, brush forwards towards the head and then sprinkle a small amount of powder in and brush

forward again, making sure the hair under the front legs is not forgotten. Do the same with the trouser hair on the back legs and flanks, taking care that you do not catch the testicles or vulva with the brush.

Gently roll the dog on to one side and start layering the coat, starting with the hair closest to the stomach. Spray, brush, powder and brush again, working in sections towards the head. After doing each side, stand the dog up and repeat the brushing process from the root of the tail up to the head. When you have brushed all the coat the wrong way, then brush it back the correct way. This will give the appearance of a stand off coat, giving plenty of body.

Do extra spraying and brushing when you get to the mane, as this is one of the most important parts of a Peke coat. The hair here is much coarser than on the body and should create a shawl right across the shoulders and neck and extend back towards the waist. The mane should be brushed upwards and forwards towards the front of the head to join in with the ears, making them look more profuse and widening the topskull.

The ear fringes should be turned back towards the head, exposing the ear lobe, and the fringes sprayed and gently combed. This is one of the few times a comb is used. Do be very gentle as those lovely black ear fringes take a long time to grow back once they have been ripped out. After combing through, flick the ears back to frame the face and brush through gently. The bib now needs spraying and powdering, brushing downwards towards the feet.

The tail is the last part of the coat to be groomed. Hold the tail in one hand and start brushing from the tip in sections down to the root so that, if there are any knots, you are not ripping through them.

When completely groomed, fan the tail out over the back. While grooming the tail keep gently spraying it as this makes it easier to groom.

AT THE SHOW

On the actual show day this grooming should be done after you have put the lead on your Peke, as putting it on afterwards just ruins all your good work.

Before going into the ring, brush his trousers flat down to his legs to create as short a body as possible. Also make sure his front leg fringes are brushed back into his sides. If these are exceptionally thick and stick out, it might be a good idea to do a bit of discreet trimming with thinning scissors but, of course, not on a show day.

Hopefully it goes without saying that his face is clean, there are no hairs in his eyes and his wrinkle is clean and dry. The line from the inner corner of the eye following the line of the wrinkle should also be quite dry. Nothing spoils the expression of a Peke as much as a wet face, so last thing, before you go into the ring, wipe the face with dry tissue.

A number of people trim the wrinkle. Do not do this on your show dog until you have practised on another dog. It should never look obvious. All you are trying to do is trim back any straggly hairs so that the eyes appear more obvious or to prevent the hair growing over the nostrils. Combing the wrinkle with a fine-tooth comb can have just the same effect. I never trim the whiskers off, but I know some breeders do. Again, this is a matter of personal choice.

When you go into the ring try to keep your hands off the coat as this will ruin the effect you have tried to achieve by spraying, powdering and brushing. Your hands contain grease which, when passed on to the coat, makes it fall flatter and so spoils the stand-off look which is part of the Pekingese glamour. Also nothing looks more impressive than a well-groomed Peke standing four-square, with his handler standing at the side or behind him – not kneeling down forever brushing his ears or tail. This spoils the whole picture and distracts the judge.

GROOMING BAG
To start with, you will only need a few items in your grooming bag.

• A good nylon and bristle brush. The best type is the Mason Pearson Junior. They are not cheap but last for years. I still have the first one we bought thirty years ago.
• A good metal comb with both fine teeth and wider teeth. I prefer the 7-inch model without a handle as this is useful when the coat is casting and you want to get as much loose dead hair out as possible.
• A pair of round-ended scissors for trimming pads without the risk of cutting the skin.
• A pair of nail-clippers. I prefer the small scissor type which are easier to use on small nails.
• Some cheap talcum powder. The supermarket brand is quite good enough, there is no need to buy a designer brand!
• A can of coat spray. There are none specifically made for Pekes like those for Poodles and it is trial and error as to which ones you feel help your dog's coat. When we started out, all these sprays were not on the market and we made up our own with rainwater and bay rum. I must admit I change sprays very often, as different dogs seem suited to different sprays.

As you become more experienced and perhaps get more dogs, you will acquire more equipment and your grooming bag will get heavier.

Show leads are things I seem to amass plenty of in various colours and thicknesses. All dog shows have trade stands that sell everything an exhibitor could ever need.

When you first start showing, stand and watch good groomers at work; do not get in the way and do not expect them to divulge their grooming secrets. They had to learn through trial and error and there is no easy way to improve except through practice. Some people never master the art, and others can make the most ordinary dog look fabulous.

If you have started at the smaller shows, by the time you have a dog good enough to go to the bigger shows, you should be able to show and present a dog to its best advantage.

TYPES OF SHOWS

Smaller shows are the training grounds, not only for dogs and handlers but also for judges. Sometimes the judge will be a breed person who has to judge so many classes of the breed before he can further his judging career by moving higher up judging lists.

When you first start showing and you do not know many people, do not be influenced by fellow exhibitors telling you which show to go to and which judge to show under. Go and find out for yourself. Remember, judging is down to how different people interpret the same Standard. What is one person's idea of small may be another's medium, but until you have shown under them you will never know.

In the US it is customary to enter your dog in one class, whereas in the UK you can, in theory, enter a dog right through from Puppy to Open. Do not be tempted to enter too many classes at first, as it could be a bit of an ordeal for your puppy while he is getting used to the strange noises and dogs, so start off in the class he is eligible for.

You cannot start showing in the US, Canada or in the UK until a puppy is six months old. In some countries it is four months, which I think is a bit young. Most breeds, especially big breeds, are very unfinished and immature at that age. Certain parts of the continent do not allow you to show puppies under nine months which does not give much time for a puppy career.

The British show scene: Ch. St Sanja Grand Finale At Yakee winning Best in Show at Midland Counties 1995.

Photo: Russell Fine Art.

The American show scene: Am. Ch. King's Court Social Lion: Top Pekingese and BIS the Pekingese Club of America Winter Specialty. Photo: Kohler.

In the UK the best way to proceed is to find out when shows are scheduled and where they are held by reading either of the two weekly dog papers, *Our Dogs* and *Dog World*. They can be ordered through your newsagent and no serious British exhibitor would be without them. Once you have started showing and winning, that is where the judges' reports are published. The AKC also publishes a list of upcoming shows and the addresses of the show superintendents in the *AKC Gazette*, a monthly magazine.

SHOW REPORTS
The UK is the only country where judges write a report on the first and second in classes and send it to the dog papers so everyone can read it a few weeks later. Not all judges do this, but it is expected. Personally, I think most of the reports are so bland, bearing very little relation to the dog in question, that they are not worth reading. Years ago judges used to describe the dogs' faults and virtues and nobody took offence. Nowadays they would probably be sued!

At Fédération Cynologique Internationale (FCI) shows (primarily in Europe and South America) the judge writes a report on every dog irrespective of whether it gets placed, and a copy is given to the exhibitor there and then. Nobody else sees what the judge has written unless the exhibitor wants to show them. These reports are usually much more constructive than ours.

ENTERING A SHOW

You have found a show not too far from home. For UK shows the secretary's name and address will be listed. Write to them requesting a schedule, enclosing a stamped self-addressed envelope. If you telephone, do not do it late at night. Secretaries do the job in an honorary capacity and have homes to run, jobs to go to and dogs to look after, so do be considerate.

When the schedule arrives it will contain an entry form which is easy to fill in as it is self-explanatory and all the details appear on your puppy's registration form. The only thing you have to think about is what class to enter.

To start with, just go into the puppy class in the breed, which means that there will only be Pekingese between the ages of six and twelve months competing with you. If there are no Pekingese classes at the show, go into the Toy Puppy classes so you will be competing with other small breeds. At AKC shows, a standard entry form is always used, and the same classes always scheduled, so you just need the name and address of the show superintendent.

Do support your local Pekingese club which usually holds its own shows each year. It is at these club shows that you will be able to talk to other Peke lovers and hopefully learn much more about the little idiosyncrasies of the breed.

When you are not grooming or showing your dog, sit at the ringside and watch how other people show their dogs. Remember, everyone is there to win, so do not expect people to tell you everything. When I first came into the breed, the top kennels were rather unapproachable and we were very grateful when they even acknowledged us and for the first few years would never dare to ask them questions.

Nowadays, people are more willing to answer queries as long as they are asked at the right time and not just as people are doing the final preparations before going into the ring.

SHOW PROCEDURE

At all levels of shows, males are judged before bitches, so, if you have a dog puppy, do allow plenty of time for your journey and give yourself time to get into the show and settle your puppy. He will probably want to go to relieve himself when he arrives. Try and ensure he does so before you groom him and go into the ring; not only is it embarrassing when a dog defecates in the ring but it can put off other dogs who want to investigate the smell.

If you have won your class, do not go wandering off as you will be needed later to compete against all the other unbeaten dogs for Best of Sex.

Nowadays, it is very rare if you win any money when you win a class. This usually only happens at breed shows. Years ago, you could often win your entry fee back. Dog showing is now an expensive hobby and you will spend more money than you get back.

By the time you feel confident that your puppy is good enough to go to a larger show, you hopefully will be more expert in presentation and handling and your dog will probably be a bit older, steadier and perhaps have already won a few prizes.

I am always amazed that some people keep going to shows for years and never win any major award. Why do they not look hard at their dogs and see how they differ from the winning dogs? This is a case of true kennel blindness; nobody has the perfect dog, but, if yours looks quite different from the ones who are winning, do something about it!

Ten years after we had started in Pekes, I realised that the line we had based our kennel on had a major fault that I was not able to breed out and so we completely changed lines and rebuilt the kennel, basing our stock on the famous Jamestown strain.

Do remember that showing is a hobby, not life and death, and that winning, although very nice, is not everything. You will still be taking the same dog home, win or lose, and never take it out on him if he has not won. It wasn't his fault, it was the judge's opinion on the day. Another day – another judge!

Never show your emotions in the ring if you have not won. You can let off steam in the privacy of the car going home. Congratulate the person whose dog has beaten yours if you think they deserve it. People always remember a bad loser and you will not do yourself any credit in the long run. Years ago, people used to sit at ringsides and comment favourably on the dogs; nowadays all you hear are people pulling the dogs to pieces and only ever remarking on their faults – never on their good points.

5 *PRINCIPLES OF BREEDING*

Some people think that because they have a bitch she must have a litter. This is an old wives' tale and there is no medical reason for bitches to be bred from. There is a chance that a maiden bitch (one never mated) can get pyometra, an infection of the womb, later in life, but this can also happen to bitches who have been bred from. If you bought your bitch just as a pet, keep her as that. Breeding Pekingese is, in my opinion, harder than breeding any other breed and the risk of things going wrong is high. We have all heard the tales of people coming down in the morning and finding mum happily nursing a litter, but we have also heard of very experienced breeders, who have been with their bitches every minute, still losing all the pups and, even worse, ending up at the vet and losing the bitch too.

If you have bought your bitch as a prospective brood and the breeder you bought her from sold her after explaining her good and bad points and showing you her pedigree (which does not have to be full of Champions but at best has some dog and kennel names you recognise), then the next task is finding a stud dog.

THE STUD DOG

I was taught by a very famous breeder to use the best dog you can for your bitch's first litter. The old-fashioned nonsense of using a local dog or a cheap dog just to 'prove' her is just that, nonsense. The first litter might be the only litter you get from your bitch, so use the best dog for her even if he lives hundreds of miles away or you have to remortgage the house for the stud fee. Hopefully, your bitch has been good enough to be shown, as there is no point in mating a poor bitch to a good dog. He can only do so much, and what is the point of producing a litter of pet-quality pups? The object of breeding is to better the breed, not to make some pin-money.

THE BROOD BITCH

It goes without saying that your bitch should be in tiptop condition. If and when your bitch is in whelp, she will give everything to her pups and, if she is lacking in body and condition, then you cannot expect the pups to do well. She must also be up to size for breeding. I would never mate a bitch under 8 lbs (3.5 kg) in weight. Under 7 lbs (3 kg) are classed as sleeve Pekes and are never, under any circumstances, used for breeding. As Pekes do not come into season regularly every six months, you cannot be hard-and-fast about not mating until, say, their third season which, in some cases, could be at eighteen months and in others at twenty-seven months. I think around eighteen months is a good time for a first litter.

If you have been to shows, you will have probably seen dogs that you have liked. Look to see how they are bred; they could have a sire in common or descend from the same family as your bitch.

BREEDING PLANS

INBREEDING

There are three kinds of breeding. Inbreeding is generally not recommended for novices, as it involves close matings such as father to daughter or brother to sister. To do this you need to know all about the dogs behind the pair and what faults and virtues they carried because, as you are not introducing any fresh blood, everything that has gone before will come out and, as well as producing very good, the bad can be awful. In the early days of the breed few came into the UK initially so I am sure there was close inbreeding, but now the gene pool is wide enough to ensure that only the very experienced would ever use inbreeding. There are not enough breeders today who have been around long enough to have enough knowledge of the dogs back in pedigrees for this method to be successful.

LINE BREEDING

This involves mating your bitch back to a dog of the same family line. Different lines will lead back to an outstanding dog who will appear five or six times in up to five generations. If the dog was dominant, his great-great-grandchildren will look like him and have his stamp. If you are only recently in the breed, you will never have seen this dog but, by studying photos and asking older breeders about him and looking at the dogs and bitches in the ring who are his descendants, you should get an idea of what he was like. Remember, no dog is perfect and his faults will be handed down as well, but, if you like the type of dog overall, it is better to go for that than a dog that excelled in coat but had a small head, for instance, if his descendants are noted for their small heads.

Family Tree for Eng. Am. Can. Dutch Asian Ch. Shiarita Emperor Roscoe

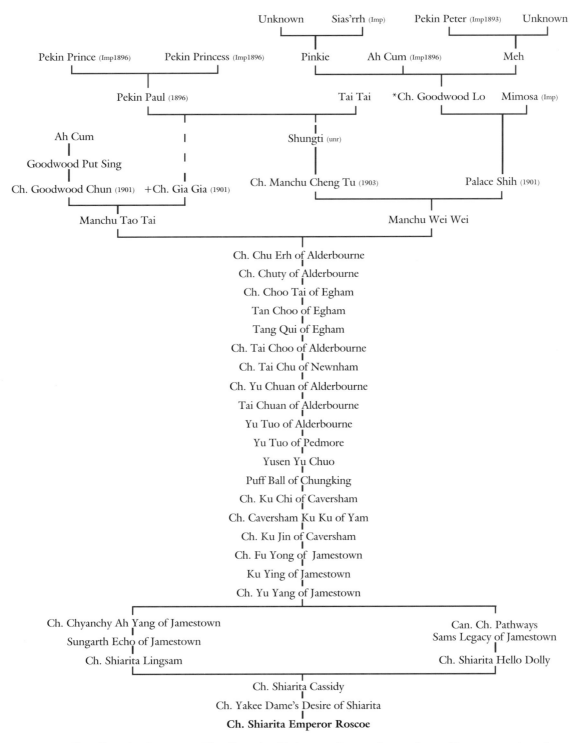

* First Champion Dog,   + First Champion Bitch,   Imp Denotes imported,   unr Denotes unregistered

Eng. Am. Can Dutch Asian Ch. Shiarita Emperor Roscoe: The most titled dog in history.

OUTCROSSING

This means mating your bitch to a dog that is not related to her as far as you can see on the pedigree. Years ago, when you could change an animal's name, it was very difficult to tell whether they were related unless you knew the history of the breed. Nowadays, when breeders are encouraged by the Kennel Club to register all puppies in a litter, it is easier to see what relation they are to each other. Even though all Pekes go back to a small number of imports, they are too far back to have any effect. Five generations on a pedigree are as much as you need to study and, while a mating may look good on paper, due to things which cannot be seen like recessive genes, there is no guarantee that you will get what you want. This all depends on the combination of genes from the dog and bitch.

UNDERSTANDING GENETICS

Genetics is a subject which can take up a whole book but, put simply, genes are what all individuals, human and animal, carry and they determine appearance and temperament. Dogs have 39 pairs of chromosomes, which are how genes are carried in the body, and, at the moment of conception, one of each comes from the sire and dam in the sperm and the egg and combine in the embryo that will be the puppy. Unfortunately, the combination is random and, although you may mate your bitch to a dog with a fantastic head, for instance, there is no guarantee that you will get all the genes that go into making that fantastic head. All the

Ch. Etive
Copplestone
Pu Zin Julier

Ch. Laparata
Celestial Star

Laparata
Celeste

Laparata
Francois

Laparata
Miranda

Laparata
Celeste

*Am. Ch. St. Aubrey Laparata Dragon: All-time top
sire of the breed in the US.   Photo: Fall.*

genes are not equal, there are dominant and recessive genes. The dominant ones are those you can see, as in the fantastic head; the recessive are those that only come out when they meet up with another of the same recessive gene. If, for instance, a dog with dark eyes carried a recessive gene for light eyes and was mated to a bitch who was the same, then some of the pups could have light eyes. But there is no way of knowing who carries what gene unless you are able to do studies of progeny by that dog and check on what he has produced. This is easier done in breeds where there are big litters but, as Pekes on average only produce two or three pups, a lot of breeding is very much hit-and-miss.

CHOOSING THE RIGHT DOG
Your selection of a stud dog should start

Ch. Copplestone Pu Zin	Ch. Copplestone Pu Zee	Ch. Copplestone Ku Zee of Loo Foo
		Sho Lo of Faygold
	Vertex Leifi	Sunlight of Minalphi
		Mary Rose of Minalphi
Pendarvis Jin Juliette of Tralee	Jin Tong of Pendarvis	Ch. Kujin of Caversham
		Poupee of Pendarvis
	Jin Julie of Tralee	Jamestown Jin Chi of Caversham
		Deidre of Tralee
Ch. Cherangani Chips	Franchard Penjinn	Ch. Kujin of Caversham
		Ch. Franchard Perracre Penanne
	Cherangani Cha Cha	Ch. Goofus Le Grisbie
		Sheraton Merrily
Laparata Ralshams Claudia	Yendis Su Yong	Ch. Fu Yong of Jamestown
		Yendis Ralshams Su Kan
	Velvet Lady of Ralsham	Pagoda Prince Rupert of Tzumaio
		Ralshams Sanctuary Grey Mist
Ch. Nathaniel of Wongville	Barnaby of Wongville	Ch. Humphrey of Wongville
		Olivia of Wongville
	Olwyn of Wongville	Oliver of Wongville
		Tytherly Megan Bach
Laparata Gay Blossom	Laparata Gay Sir	Ch. Cherangani Chips
		Laparata Ralshams Claudia
	Yu Peach of Devana	Ch. Linsown Ku Che Tu
		Tia Maria of Devana
Ch. Cherangani Chips	Franchard Penjinn	Ch. Ku Jin of Caversham
		Ch. Franchard Perracre Penanne
	Cherangani Cha Cha	Ch. Goofus Le Grisbie
		Sheraton Merrily
Laparata Ralshams Claudia	Yendis Su Yong	Ch. Fu Yong of Jamestown
		Yendis Ralshams Su Kan
	Velvet Lady of Ralsham	Pagoda Prince Rupert of Tzumaio
		Ralsham Sanctuary Grey Mist

many months before your bitch is due to be mated by seeing dogs in the show ring and by being guided by the breeder of your bitch. Do not be tempted to use a dog in a pet home such as one owned by a relative. Mating does not come naturally to Pekes and they need manual assistance. It could alter a pet dog's temperament and have him lifting his leg all over the house and practising on human legs. Stud work in Pekes is quite involved and even some of the more experienced breeders use an outside person to help at mating times.

Because of the Peke's shape with its short legs and wide, deep chest, the males do not have an easy time getting on to a bitch and getting into the right position, so preferably two people need to assist, one at the head end of the bitch to make sure she does not move about and, more importantly, does not turn around and snap at the dog when he finally penetrates. Years ago, we used to do the matings on the floor, but long ties and creaky knees now mean that, for comfort, we do it on a worktop or, in our case, the top of a chest freezer.

When taking your bitch to a stud dog, especially if he is one that is used regularly, do inform the owner well before your bitch is in season that you would like to use him. Most responsible stud dog owners want to see the pedigree of your bitch beforehand and possibly see the bitch herself. Most dogs are only at stud to approved bitches and it is the stud dog owner who approves of the bitch or not. If the stud dog owner has had quite a bit of experience in the breed and knows something of your bitch's pedigree, he/she will be able to advise you on whether that particular dog will be suitable for your bitch.

Once you have decided on a stud dog, and his owner has agreed and told you the stud fee and any other conditions there may be, such as how many matings and whether there is a free mating if the bitch misses, it is up to you to watch for when your bitch comes into season and let the stud owner know right away so the dog can be kept available.

Some stud dog owners want the bitch to be swabbed by the vet to check that she does not have a streptococcus infection and, although it will not do any harm, it can stop her having pups or mean she will have a much smaller litter. It can also be passed on to the stud dog and live on him for a few days, so he could pass it to another bitch if he is used afterwards. The vet will swab her when she comes into season and can give her drugs to clear the infection in a few days. She can then be safely mated.

READY FOR MATING

Start looking at your bitch's vulva well before you think she is due to come in season because, although the books say every six months, most bitches and certainly Pekes have never read those books! They vary from six-month gaps to twelve months. There are some who come in every four months, but I would hesitate to breed from these as usually there is some uterine problem and I would be inclined to have these bitches spayed.

The first signs are swelling and then bleeding. If your bitch is able to get around to her genital area and clean it, you may miss the beginning of bleeding, so it is important that you look at her bedding first thing in the morning before she goes out and gently wipe the surface of her vulva with a tissue to check for colour. It is important to know when day one of bleeding was so you can inform the stud's owner on which day you will be coming. The rule of thumb is to mate on day eleven and thirteen. Again, all bitches are different and I have mated bitches as early as day seven and as late

Eng. Ir. Ch. Shiarita Fort Lauderdale: Sire of Ch. Shiarita Cassidy.

Ch. Shiarita Cassidy: Top British Pekingese 1978, 1979, 1980; Top Sire 1979-1981, 1985 and 1989.

as day twenty one and they have-produced pups. There are some external signs which can give you a clue as to when your bitch is ready; the discharge changes from red to pink and then colourless, the vulva is very soft and quite enlarged and, if you run your finger down her spine, her tail will flag to one side leaving her genital area totally accessible to the stud.

Some bitches may bleed for all of the three weeks and be fertile for all that time, so mating and breeding is still quite a hit-and-miss business. Assuming your bitch is normal and, at the

eleventh day, colour has finished, she is very swollen and flicking her tail from side to side, off you go to the stud dog.

If the dog lives a long distance away, do find out from the stud dog owner whether you will be able to leave her there for the second mating. Although this does not save you anything in travelling time and costs, it can sometimes be more settling for the bitch. If your bitch has never been away from home before, see if you can take her a few days beforehand to give her time to settle in.

Up until the 1980s, it was common

Am. Ch. St Aubrey Sunburst Of Elsdon: A key sire in North American pedigrees.

Photo: Booth.

for people to send their bitches by train. The stud dog owners collected them at their local station, kept them for a few days, mated them twice and sent them back the same way. Suddenly the cost of this service escalated so much that most of the travelling is now done by car and bitches are handed over at shows or some mutually convenient spot if they are not taken the whole journey.

TESTING FOR OVULATION

As mating is such a hit-and-miss business and often includes high

travelling costs as well as the stud fee, it is not surprising that there are now one or two tests you can have done on your bitch to determine the day she starts ovulating. Vaginal smears are usually done by the vet and necessitate the bitch being taken to the surgery on about day four or five, to start with. The vet uses a sterile cotton swab or similar impliment and inserts it in the vagina for about four to five inches until it reaches the cervix. It is rotated for one full turn and then withdrawn. The swab is rolled on to a slide and stained with methylene blue or similar agent, then the slide is put under the microscope to be read.

Simply, what the vet is looking for are higher levels of progesterone and luteinizing hormone which indicate ovulation. It does mean that smears will have to be taken every forty-eight hours over a period of days before they can tell you the right time for mating. About eight days after the start of pro-oestrus (heat) in a normal bitch, the LH levels peak and oestrogen levels drop while the progesterone is still rising. At this time, which is oestrus, the surge of LH causes ovulation and the eggs are released over a period of no more than 24 hours. Although ovulation occurs, on average, ten to twelve days after the start of bleeding, this can vary from seven to twenty-five days. Four days after ovulation the eggs are ready for fertilization and if they are not fertilized within thirty-six hours they die and the

Ch. Lotusgrange Again The Same: Son of Ch. Some Man Of Lotusgrange.

Photo: Anne Roslin-Williams.

Ch. Some Man Of Lotusgrange.

Photo: Anne Roslin-Williams.

bitch will miss. A male's sperm can live in a bitch for forty-eight hours, and sometimes bitches are mated and have good ties before the eggs are ready for fertilization, which can often mean breeders think their bitches have gone over time. A bitch will stand for a dog for a few days before actual conception time, so, unless you know the actual date of conception, sixty-three days of pregnancy is only a rough estimate.

Another test for the optimum time for mating involves the vet taking blood samples, putting them in a centrifuge, adding pre-developed lotions and reading the levels of progesterone. I have used this test on a number of occasions and have had litters born from matings as early as the seventh day to as late as the twenty-fifth. Bitches can often be different at their next season.

If you are using an outside stud dog, it would be good manners to let the owner know that you are having your bitch tested as you might have to take her to the dog earlier or later in her season than had been expected. This might be inconvenient, especially if the stud dog is also being shown, because not everyone wants a mating the day before a show. Males often go off their food when an in-season bitch is around, or spend their time in the ring with their noses to the ground.

KEEPING A STUD DOG

In my opinion, until you have done some breeding and winning with home-bred stock, there is no reason to keep your own stud dog. The very best dogs carrying the top lines are available to every breeder for the cost of a stud fee and travel expenses. To breed, keep and show a male that is worthy of being a stud dog and has something to pass on, costs a lot more than a number of stud fees to the top studs available.

Any male can sire, and often they sire stock that can do a bit of winning at a lower level, but that does not make them a good stud dog. A good stud dog, to my mind, is one who sires stock which are successful in the ring at Championship level and beyond, whose progeny look something like him and who, in turn, produce winning progeny. He himself does not have to be a Champion, as Champions do not always produce Champions, but looking at any line-bred pedigree you will see that, more often than not, the prepotent and dominant dogs who made an impression on the breed at any stage were also winners in their own right.

THE MATING

If you do decide to use your own stud dog, you will know from going to outside studs that the actual process of mating is not that easy. Firstly, do the mating somewhere quiet with no other dogs around getting interested. If you are using a tabletop, make sure it is not slippery. We use a rubber car mat so the dog can keep his grip, as he will only

Am. Ch. St. Aubrey Melba of Elsdon: Top producing dam.

have his back feet on the ground most of the time.

Let the pair meet each other on the floor so that they have time to do a little flirting. If the bitch is ready or nearly so, she will dance around the stud dog flicking her tail from side to side and encouraging him. Older proven broods will often push their back ends right into the dog's face very suggestively. I would not advise doing the mating in your lounge as the males usually lift their legs a number of times during this courtship, both through excitement and for scent-marking their territory.

It is easier to have two people to assist at a mating, certainly until you are very experienced, and I would always advise two people to handle a young inexperienced stud dog. The last thing you need is a bitch turning round and snapping at him.

Stand the bitch firmly on the table, making sure she cannot wriggle about or turn around. If she has lots of hair in her skirts, part them so the way is easier for the dog to get in. If I am mating on my own, I gather the bitch's skirts in two bunches and put them in elastic bands, so both I and the dog can work easily. Before lifting the dog on to the table I insert a well-lubricated gloved finger in her vagina to make sure she is well open and to provide an easy passage for the dog's penis.

An experienced male will probably jump straight on to the bitch but younger, less experienced males might have to be lifted on. The person who is at the working end should have their left hand under the bitch with their second and third fingers either side of the vulva. This enables you to feel whether the dog has gone in and not

77

Ch. Singlewell T'Sai Magic: Winner of 15 CCs, and dam of Ch. Singlewell Magic Charm, Ch. Singlewell Some Magic, Ch. Singlewell Sensation, Ch. Singlewell Magic Ruler.

Ch. Yakee Charm School Deb: Dam of Ch. Yakee Got Wot It Takes and Ch. Yakee All Eyes On Me. Photo: Lindsay.

Ch. Yakee Got Wot It Takes: Twice BOB at Crufts. Photo: Trafford.

aimed too high or to one side. A dog who is used to this will tend to aim for your fingers and start serious pushing when he feels them. Dogs will often enter bitches a few times before seriously thrusting. Sometimes, due to their short legs and wide ribcages, they may have difficulty in getting at the right angle, and so a pile of newspapers or a telephone directory should be positioned under the mating mat to give a bit of elevation. Because of the shape of the pelvic girdle the dog's penis will have to enter slightly upwards so this is another reason for the elevation. The dog will grasp the bitch's waist tightly with his front legs and the stud dog handler will sometimes have to guide the penis to the vulva or vice versa. When he starts thrusting, a gentle hand on his rear can just help to hold him in as he starts swelling.

THE TIE

There are three stages of ejaculation. The first is just clearing out any urine from the penis; the second, which is when the dog makes strong thrusting motions and hunches himself up, contains the sperm; the third contains clear liquids which speed the sperm up to the waiting eggs. The tie occurs when the sperm is released and is caused by the swelling of the bulb glands on the penis and the bitch's vaginal muscles constricting. Once this occurs, there is no way of separating them until she releases him – so be prepared to settle down for a long wait. Ties can last from a couple of minutes to an hour, so you can see why I prefer mating on a worktop. Once a pair are firmly tied, it is easier on the bitch's back if the dog is turned. Hold the bitch still and help the dog lift one of his back legs over her back so they are standing rear to rear. Hold their tails together or their back legs to prevent them moving about. Talk to them quietly to make sure there are no sudden movements, as it would be very painful to both and there could be internal damage.

When the tie has finished, put the bitch in a pen or travelling box to keep her quiet and still for at least half an hour. Examine the male to make sure his penis has retracted fully and that he has not got any hairs from the sheath caught inside. I wipe over with a cold wet cloth as this can often get things back in place quickly.

Do not worry if you do not get a tie, as it is not necessary to get a bitch pregnant, but it does increase the chances and I am one of the old school who prefer one. If you get an outside tie when the swelling is outside of the vagina, hold both of them together until ejaculation is finished to stop the semen leaking out.

FURTHER MATINGS

For a normal bitch, two matings forty-eight hours apart should be enough if you have hit on the right day. If in doubt or the bitch has a history of misses or single pups, then it will do the dog no harm to mate her every other day for a week. The stud dog should not be expected to do this on a regular basis as excessive use can lower fertility.

When taking your bitch to an outside stud, do find out from the owner beforehand how many matings your bitch is going to get, as some famous stud dogs are only used once on a bitch. Remember, the stud fee is only for the service, not the result, and, if the bitch misses, it is at the stud dog owner's discretion whether you get a free service.

Sometimes a maiden bitch will have a vaginal obstruction like a hymen which will need to be broken down. An experienced stud dog will do this himself with a few well-aimed thrusts, otherwise it is better done before the bitch gets to meet the dog so as not to upset her. This is done with a well-lubricated finger gently inserted in the vulva.

HELPING HANDS

Stud work with Pekingese is not easy and the stud dog owner should be informed right at the beginning of the season, not just because the dog might not be available, but because they might need to contact a handler. Likewise, if you are doing your own mating, it does really need two people, one at the head end to hold and calm the dog. Often a stud can take quite a while before he actually gets there and will hop on and off having a few thrusts before he decides everything is right.

Pekingese stud work is not something you do just before you go out to dinner. Some Pekes will only do it after a bit of playing about and flirting and they will not be hurried up. Others will have a few goes, jumping on and off the bitch and playing about before they finally decide that they mean business. If they do not show much interest, be guided by them. They know when the time is right. The bitch must give off some hormonal scent when she is just right and although, in the past, the rule of thumb has been mating on the eleventh and thirteenth day, the increased use of tests which tell exactly when a bitch is ovulating means we are mating earlier and being more accurate.

As the sperm can live in the bitch for a number of days, it is possible that it can be there waiting for the bitch to ovulate or waiting for the eggs to mature. Often, when bitches are said to go over their time, it is really because the sperm has not met up with eggs that are ready on the day of mating, so pregnancy can seem to last between fifty-eight and seventy-two days, depending on when the mature eggs met up with the sperm.

PEAK CONDITION

It goes without saying that a dog being used at stud should be physically fit and free from any infection, internal or external. This is not just at the time of mating but throughout his stud life, as sperm is made several months previously and a number of factors can affect it. An illness months previously can affect the production of sperm, especially one where steroids were used or the dog had periods of high temperature.

Some dogs can become sterile at three or four years old, while others can still sire at ten or eleven.

After the mating, do make sure you get a signed form from the stud dog owner at the time of payment of the stud fee and be aware of any details of repeat matings or free services.

6 PREGNANCY AND WHELPING

My first advice to would-be breeders of Pekingese is – forget it! Pekingese are a difficult whelping breed and, if every breeder of any breed had to whelp a litter of Pekes first, then at least a third of them would give up.

Hopefully the previous chapter on choosing a stud dog and the actual mating has been of some use and your bitch has gone six weeks from the date of mating. She should have a normal life in that time, fresh air, exercise and the same amount of food as usual. If she is normally very active and jumps on and off chairs or the settee, I would try to curb that, but otherwise treat her normally. Pregnancy is not an illness. Often it is difficult to tell whether a Peke is pregnant up to six or even seven weeks, especially if she only has one puppy, as she can keep it tucked well up in the womb. Pekes do not have many pups and I have found the more line-bred they are, the smaller the litter size.

When she shows in whelp, from six weeks onwards, you should increase her food, giving her extra protein in the form of eggs, cheese and chicken. Four or five small meals are better than two large ones because the womb full of pups presses on the stomach and pregnant bitches can only eat small amounts.

THE LAST THREE WEEKS

At six to seven weeks the teats become a deeper pink, due to increased blood supply, and are enlarged. You notice this more in the pair near the back legs, as these usually are the ones most used by the pups.

She will often have a white mucous discharge from the vagina; this is usually indicative of her being in whelp. Only worry when this has blood or any colour in it. She will want to relieve herself more often as a full uterus pressing on the bladder means she will not be able to hold on for as long as usual and, if she is house-trained, you might have to get up and let her out during the night.

If she is a maiden bitch or your only one who lives in the house, sits on the chairs and sleeps on the bed, you should introduce her to her whelping quarters no more than eight weeks after the first mating. This should be in a quiet and draughtproof area away from other dogs and the normal activity of the household. Some people use a spare bedroom or a downstairs room that is not in everyday use.

In the old days breeders used a large cardboard box which could be disposed of afterwards, but now there are so many manufactured whelping boxes on the market that it is more sensible to lay out the money for one of these which will probably last you all your breeding life. Peke puppies need heat for the first two weeks even in summer and there are many heating pads on the market. These have been especially made for dogs and are chewproof and thermostatically controlled. Do not use overhead infrared lamps. Pups can move away from under the heat and soon get chilled, and I do not think they are very safe for Pekes' eyes.

Do be careful in picking up and carrying your heavily pregnant bitch. It goes without saying that she should never be picked up by her front legs but, at this stage, she should not be picked up by the scruff of her neck either. Support her heavy tummy with one hand while holding her under her chest with the other in the normal way. All bitches are different in their whelping patterns and, just because someone told you that you will know when they have started because they scratch up and pant, do not be fooled by this. Never go off and leave them from about their fifty-sixth day after mating. Many a litter has been born at fifty-seven days and lived. Bitches can also go for up to seventy days after mating as the day of mating, may not be the day of conception. It is also untrue that they will not whelp if they have eaten. I have bitches who had their first pups half an hour after a good meal.

THE LAST FEW DAYS

I allow a pregnant bitch to sleep next to my bed a week before the sixty-third day and I take her temperature regularly during that time. The easiest thermometer to use is one of the digital type which bleeps when the temperature has reached the correct level and relays the figure on to a screen. Do be very gentle when inserting the thermometer into the anus. I lightly moisten it so that it is not so hard and dry.

The normal canine temperature is 38.5 degrees Centigrade (101.3 degrees Fahrenheit). My rule of thumb is that if it is between 37 and 38.5 degrees C nothing will happen for the next twelve hours so you can go to bed or nip to the shops, depending on the hour of day or night. As the bitch's temperature is lower than normal in the last week before whelping, you need to take it twice a day to know when it drops below 37 degrees C. Whelping usually takes place within twenty-four hours of this final drop. In my experience it is usually night, even if you mate during the day. It makes no difference – when body resistance is low, about 3am, then whelping will start seriously. Unfortunately that is when your resistance is low as well, but you have got to be strong, as Peke bitches depend on you during whelping as well as at mating time.

Whelping is something they need help with, usually a lot of help, and quite often veterinary help. It goes without saying that your vet should have been informed about your bitch's pregnancy from the moment you knew she was definitely in whelp. Normally there is no need for the bitch to go to the surgery during pregnancy unless she becomes ill. I have never seen the need for a vet to tell me how many pups a bitch is having.

Make sure you know how to contact your vet outside of surgery hours.

THE WHELPING
There are some bitches who are silent whelpers and these can often be more distressing than bitches who spend hours scratching, panting and pacing about, because at least with the latter you can see that something is going to happen. Silent whelpers hardly give a ripple when sliding a pup out, which they then leave in the bag to drown, if you are not sitting right beside the whelping box and lifting their tails up regularly. Most Pekes find it difficult to break the bag of membranes surrounding a pup, due to their flat face and lack of muzzle, and, if the bag is not removed quickly, the pup will suffocate – so bitches need the intervention of a human to tear it off, get the pup breathing air and inflate the lungs. The bag is made up of two layers of membrane and can be very strong so do not be too gentle about breaking it. Remember speed is essential.

THE FIRST STAGE
There are three stages of labour. The first stage is hardly noticeable in some bitches, but this is when the temperature drops and the pup starts its journey from the womb down to the vagina. The puppies, not the dam, start off the whelping process as they become crowded in the womb and the stress of this stimulates the whelping process in the bitch. She will become restless and confused and do things which are out of character. Do make sure she is spending most of the time in the whelping box and not roaming about the house as she may decide to whelp in a dark, quiet place which might turn out to be under a bed or an armchair!

This restless behaviour can last up to

forty-eight hours in some bitches and I have had phone calls from first-time breeders wanting to know if all was well and was their bitch having problems. Every whelping is different, even with the same bitch. The paper tearing is more to do with a reaction to pain than bed making and a bitch may do it between puppies. Some bitches never do any of this and have a perfect, normal whelping. It does not mean they are going to have inertia. Sometimes you will see the plug of mucus dissolve and the waters break but, again, do not worry if you see none of this.

SECOND STAGE

Second stage labour shows in the strong muscular contractions which look as though ripples are running through the body. Often the bitch will stand up and look as though she is relieving herself. Bitches will often become vocal as the contractions can be painful, as in labour pains, and some will yelp or growl. Second stage labour and the gap between pups being born can go on for quite a while, sometimes as long as thirty-six hours! Yes, you have probably read the books that say if bitches have been pushing for two hours with no result then you must get veterinary help. It is the strength and number of pushes which exhaust a bitch, not the length of time in between them. Some bitches are slow and sluggish whelpers and will do a bit of half-hearted pushing and scratching up and then lie down

and go to sleep for a couple of hours. They can do this for a day and a night and, as long as they are resting in between contractions and are not tiring themselves, then there is no cause for alarm. You tend to know your own bitches after a couple of litters and it is useful to write a few notes on each whelping in the early days.

The cervix must dilate to allow the pups to travel from the uterus down the vagina and out. Do not try to find this out by sticking your finger up her vagina; it is very difficult to tell anyway unless you are very experienced, and you might cause damage to the first unborn pup and pain to the bitch who can often turn round and bite you.

THE BIRTH

In an ideal whelping the pups would be born head first but, because of the shape of a Peke (i.e. the big head, wide shoulders and narrow rear end), this can often cause as much trouble as a rear end presentation. It is vital that the first pup does not get stuck, because it will hold up those behind whose placentas will have started separating from the walls of the uterus and who will need to breathe outside of the bitch's womb as soon as possible. Often you will see a dark fluid-filled sack commonly called the water bag. This is the amniotic sac which has surrounded each pup through pregnancy and now helps it to slide out more easily. Do not worry if it bursts or appears and disappears a few

THE WHELPING PROCESS

1. The birth of the first puppy which is still attached to the placenta. The sac has been broken open so the pup can breathe. The mother will eat the placenta.

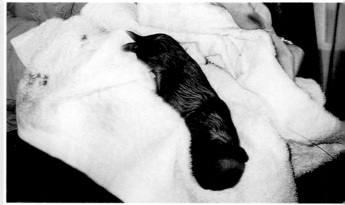

4. The puppy has now been thoroughly dried.

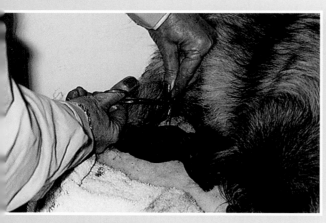

2. At this stage, the placenta is still inside the dam, but the cord is being cut.

5. The bitch has finished whelping after producing four puppies.

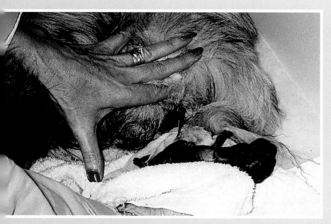

3. The puppy is being rubbed dry while the mother prepares for the next push to expel the placenta.

6. The puppies are feeding contentedly.

times; there is not a puppy in it, it just heralds a puppy's imminent arrival.

Some bitches will stand up and push really hard, whereas others lie down and hardly look as if they are putting any effort into it. Do not panic if a contraction produces half of the pup still in its membrane or bag and the bitch seems to stop; it is quite physical work and they are just gathering strength for the next strong contraction. Remember all those TV programmes of women giving birth, sweat pouring from the hard physical effort and everyone standing around and shouting at her to push! I have heard myself doing the same to a bitch and getting really agitated.

A LITTLE HELP

Sometimes you have to help, otherwise you will lose that pup and maybe the ones behind. If the next contraction has not expelled any more of the pup and you fear that the bitch is giving up for one reason or another, be prepared to help pull it out. Your hands should be well scrubbed, or you can use thin surgical gloves. I was advised years ago to use rough towelling, but I found it tore off the bag and then the need for speed was more urgent as the pup had no protection, especially if it was hindlegs first, as it would suffocate.

Holding the pup between your first two fingers with your hand facing down and waiting until the bitch pushes again, gently pull at the same time, using a downward movement. It is often useful to have lubricating jelly handy at this time and smear it around the edge of the vagina to help the pup slide out. Only pull when the bitch is pushing and do not pull out in a straight line, always pull downwards. I find in Pekes that most pups are born hindlegs first and the head and shoulders get stuck, so you need to gently insert a well-lubricated finger and try to turn them slightly. Often this is all it needs to slide out on the next push.

Try to stay calm, as panicking only upsets the bitch and you have no time to get help from the vet so it is down to you. A slight turn of the puppy is sometimes all that is needed, plus a gentle pull when she is pushing. It is no help to pull when she is not straining. Sometimes you will see the back legs moving in the bag but, by the time you have got it out, because the head or shoulders have got stuck, the puppy is dead. Do try resuscitating it by holding it upside down and swinging it to get any fluid out of its nose and lungs. Try anything – mouth to mouth, brandy on its tongue, rubbing it, anything you have ever read or been told. Ninety per cent of the time it will be useless, as I know, having had the frustration of seeing movement in the sac but, after pulling and screaming at the bitch to push, tried everything to no avail. Do not pull hard on just the legs or the head. Try to be patient until a little more of the puppy appears for you to get hold of.

Sometimes the effort a bitch puts into her contractions with nothing alive to show for it makes me think that the Americans have got the right idea in usually choosing pre-elective Caesarians. The idea is that there are no sleepless nights beforehand, the bitch is not worn out and you do not lose pups. As Pekes have small litters generally there is a lot to be said for this, for there is nothing more upsetting for bitch and owner to lose one or two pups which might be half or even all of the litter.

THE PUP ARRIVES
Once your bitch has had a pup, either easily or with your help, the first thing to do is break the bag by tearing it with your nails. The pup must breathe fresh air as soon as possible. Always have plenty of old towels handy and, holding the pup upside down, rub it with a towel quite firmly, not gently patting. This not only stimulates the lungs to expand and drains the fluid, but helps natural breathing. Let the bitch see you doing this as she will get distressed if the pup is taken out of sight. Do not be in too much of a hurry to cut the cord. Once the pup has given a cry or two and is a bit drier, then gently squeeze the cord with two fingers about one inch from the pup's stomach and cut with sterilised round-ended scissors. You do not need to do anything else with the cord. It does not need tying or clamping. There might still be some

blood coming from it. This is only the residue from the placenta, which has been the food line all the time the pup has been in the womb. If the cord is still attached to the placenta and that is still inside the vulva, do not worry. The main thing is to open the sac and get the puppy breathing. If the pup needs its airways clearing and it is impossible to do so while it is still attached in this way, then squeeze and cut the cord. Each pup does not have to be born with its placenta; they can come separately.

Let the bitch have the pup as soon as possible, even if she has not finished whelping. The licking is said to stimulate the birth process and most bitches get agitated if they have not got the pup with them and tend to hold off the birth of the next one.

I always let bitches have the afterbirth (placenta) to eat as it helps the milk flow. They are very nutritious and full of blood, but they will give the bitch very dark, runny motions, so if you have a big litter I would restrict her to no more than two. Do not worry if they do not appear with each pup; they can often come away a day later when the bitch is urinating. A retained placenta can make a bitch ill, so watch out for restlessness, lack of concentration on the pups, high temperature, not eating and a foul-smelling discharge. Many breeders routinely ask the vet to give an oxytocin injection after whelping in order to clear the virus.

At three days of age, the puppies, sleeping on their heat-pad, are making good progress.

CARE OF THE NEWBORN PUPS

At the side of the whelping box I have a polystyrene box into which I put a white polyester fur base and a heating pad. The boxes I get from a pet shop which takes delivery of fish in them. They tend to keep the heat in, and the first pups are put in there when the bitch starts serious pushing again. You also need a good supply of newspapers as Peke whelping, in my experience, is the wettest and dirtiest of all breeds. Do not be worried if everything turns

green. This is the broken-down blood from the placenta which stains everything, especially under your nails which you need to scrub for the next two days. It does wash out from towels and bedding but, initially, leaves them all a lovely shade of pale green!

The only time you need to worry about the green is if you see it before any pups are born, as this means they have separated from the walls of the womb and it is best that your vet sees the bitch quickly.

Let the pups suckle as soon as possible, as this first milk is very important. It is the colostrum containing all the antibodies which the bitch passes on to the pups to give them protection in the first few weeks of life. Suckling also stimulates contractions, so each pup is helping its brother or sister into the world. Often the teats do not look very swollen but the milk is there in the glands and needs a puppy to suck to bring it down.

I have often heard breeders say that they have had to supplement pups because there was not enough milk. I think this causes more harm than good because, if a pup is getting a full tummy from another source, it is not going to suckle so the bitch will start to dry up. In my opinion there are very few bitches who do not have enough milk to feed a normal Peke-sized litter. A puppy that is having milk from two different sources is more inclined to have an upset tummy which can cause colic and the terrible crying that goes with it.

THE INTERVAL BETWEEN PUPS
The interval between the birth of puppies is a difficult thing to gauge and cannot be learnt from reading a book. If two hours have gone by since the last pup and the bitch has been straining fairly regularly with strong pushes and no sign of anything, then you should be on your way to the vet. If you have bred a few litters and know the history of your bitch's previous whelpings, then you will probably be on your way to the vet before this point. Sometimes all it takes is an injection of oxytocin and, minutes later, a pup is born in the surgery or in the car on the way home.

If the bitch has been lying restfully most of the time since the last pup and only occasionally giving gentle pushes, then I would let her carry on until she is ready. I find that Pekingese whelpings can often be long-drawn-out events. If she has had three or four pups and then a long break and seems quite settled and the pups are feeding well, it could be that she is finished. Often, after a good-sized litter, it is hard to tell as the uterus is still quite swollen and can give the appearance of still holding puppies. You will not be the first person who has sat by the whelping box for hours thinking there is still more to come.

INERTIA
Some bitches do not respond after an injection of oxytocin. This is classed as secondary uterine inertia and is due to the uterine muscles becoming too tired to do any more. The answer is a Caesarian section, quite a commonplace event nowadays. Due to better anaesthetics and vets having more experience of doing Caesarians, the high fatalities in bitches belong to the past. This is not to say that a section is foolproof and to be undertaken lightly. We have all heard of people losing bitches on the table, however good the vet is or how fit the bitch was. It is very upsetting for owner and vet – and I speak from experience. Usually the heart gives out just as the vet is stitching up.

In primary uterine inertia, when the bitch shows no sign of pushing at all, then a Caesarian is the only answer. Primary inertia can often happen when there is only one puppy and there is not enough of the hormone produced which starts off whelping. I personally would never allow more than two Caesarians on any bitch and would ask my vet to spay her on the second one. Then I would find her a suitable pet home.

There is nothing more aggravating than having two pups naturally and then having to have a Caesarian for a dead one, not only because it puts the bitch at risk, however good your vet is. She is also going to have quite a tender stomach for a while, it will reduce her breeding life as you should leave at least twelve months gap before breeding from her again, and, lastly, it is expensive.

If you have to go to the surgery during whelping, leave the newborn pups at home, preferably in something like a polystyrene box which holds the heat and on a heating pad. Their most important need in the first few hours is warmth; they can manage without food for a few hours although, being a bit of a pessimist, I always make sure they have had some milk from the bitch because of that precious colostrum, just in case something awful happens to her.

PROBLEMS

Do check all pups for cleft palate and harelips. These are two defects which are more common in brachycephalic breeds (flat-faced). Open the pup's mouth and feel the roof of the mouth with your little finger. In a cleft palate, the roof of the mouth has not joined together and I am afraid the only answer is for the pup to be put to sleep. Often cleft palates are accompanied by harelips when there is a gap between the nostrils and the top lip. A harelip can sometimes be operated on when the pup is older, but the affected pup needs careful management before then to ensure that it is getting enough nourishment.

A cleft palate that is too fine to be seen or felt will often reveal itself, as the pup will have milk coming down its nose and will cry and look thinner than its littermates because it will not be getting enough nourishment.

CARE OF THE DAM

To make it easier for the pups to suckle, I trim the hair around the teats but, otherwise, the bitch has had normal grooming during pregnancy. After whelping is completed and she has relieved herself, I do wash her trousers, having once had a puppy strangle in a mother's skirts which had gone hard and stringy and had looped around the pup's neck. So keeping them washed and dried means that they are still presentable, but are not a danger to any puppy that wanders into them. I must admit the sight of a bitch's coat completely cut down for whelping does distress me. A Peke is a coated breed; that is one of its charms, so why cut all their coat off? If you cannot spare the time to keep them clean and tidy, should you be breeding, as it is a very time-consuming job?

A bitch that has had to have a Caesarian will have had all her tummy shaved and possibly a large section of her flank, depending on where the vet has made the incision.

CAESARIAN BIRTH

If you have to take your bitch to the veterinary surgery with complications which might lead to a Caesarian, do not take any pups already born. There is no need for the vet to see them if they are healthy and have no obvious problems.

Leave them in a warm box on the heat pad and out of any draughts. Also remember if you have other animals in the house to make sure there is no way they can get to the pups while you are away. An experienced brood bitch will hear pups crying and do her best to get to them wherever they are in the house, not always with the best intentions though. Not every mother loves another's offspring.

Modern anaesthetics mean that a bitch is awake soon after the operation is over and, however many pups the vet has to get out, the whole thing from giving her the anaesthetic to stitching her up and bringing her round should not be longer than half an hour. Sometimes the vet will give her a shot of oxytocin first if he can feel a pup very close to presentation, but, after an internal examination, he will know whether a Caesarian is the only option.

Unless you have a very good relationship with your vet and he is sure you are not going to pass out or get in the way, you will be asked to wait in the waiting room and the pups will be brought to you. If you are asked to go home and come back in a few hours to pick up the bitch and her puppies, politely decline and say that you would like to have the pups as soon as possible. I find that veterinary nurses are never rough enough with the pups and only want to gently pat them dry instead of copying the mother and really knocking them about to stimulate

breathing and clear the nose and airways. So sit there in the waiting room with your rough towels and the polystyrene box with a hot water bottle so they do not have too much change of temperature. Give each pup a good rub, holding it upside down and rubbing gently around the nose to clear away any mucus. There is no nicer sound than that first strong cry of a newborn puppy.

Puppies born by Caesarian are often a little less active due to some of the anaesthetic getting to them, but this soon wears off.

AFTERCARE

When travelling home from the surgery, keep the bitch and her puppies apart. A mother, especially a first-timer, might be a bit shocked to have little bodies crawling all over her very tender tummy. I generally put the bitch in the whelping box to have a sleep and keep the pups separate and warm so they are quiet. A puppy can manage for quite a few hours without nourishment, but will become very distressed if cold.

When the bitch seems more alert, introduce one pup at a time to her and watch her reaction before putting the others in. If she has had a litter before, she will tuck them under her and nurse them normally, even with a line of stitches down her middle. A first-timer will be a bit more wary, so sit with her all the time. This is when you need a helper who can relieve you because, sometimes, with an unsettled mother, she might need constant attendance for a few days and nights. I learnt this to my cost many years ago when a bitch had to have a Caesarian due to an obstruction and, after coming home and having a rest, she seemed to take to her pups and let them suckle and she washed and nursed them. After sitting with her for a few hours, I went into the next room to get her some food and moments later returned to find she had quietly bitten both their heads off. Now, if there is nobody to relieve me and I have to move away from the box containing any bitch I have the slightest doubt about, I take the pups away and pop them in the ever-present polystyrene box.

The wound itself should not need any attention, but keep your eye on it to see that hair does not get caught up in the stitches or that any weeping occurs. If you have to wash the tummy and wound area, use only a very mild antiseptic so as not to put the pups off sucking or to sting a very sensitive area. The stitches are usually removed seven to ten days after the operation and, when taking your bitch back to the surgery, make sure she is warm and take her in a travelling box with your own towel to put on the examining table to minimise the chance of picking up an infection and bringing it home to the pups.

The vet will have given your bitch a shot of antibiotics after the operation and will have given you a course of antibiotic tablets to give to her for a prescribed course. Do make sure she takes these as, even if she has had no contact with other dogs and goes out to relieve herself in a safe area in your garden, she is still open to picking up an infection.

There are a number of reasons that a bitch might need a Caesarian: a badly presented pup (often caused by a head being tucked under and presenting the shoulders, coming down one horn, missing the cervix and going up the other horn), uterine inertia, a dead pup or a very big pup. Your vet will tell you the reasons this time, and from these you should determine whether there will be a next time for this bitch.

FALSE PREGNANCY
Although it is distressing to the bitch and sometimes more so to the owner, a false or phantom pregnancy is quite normal in dogs, unlike most other mammals. It is believed that over 60 per cent of bitches have false pregnancies and it is to do with them living in packs in the wild. As there were often a number of bitches mated at the same time, the others, who had come on heat but had not been mated, carried on with hormone changes, giving the appearance of pregnancy; swollen teats and producing milk. In a pack it was useful to have extra bitches with milk to feed a large number of pups.

In a home environment it can be a nuisance, as the bitch gets quiet and twitchy and wants to take toys to bed. Nearer to the time when she thinks she is going to have pups, she might start ripping up and bed making. In mild cases, it is better just to ignore it and reduce her liquid intake so she does not make as much milk. In more severe cases, the vet might need to give hormone injections and perhaps spay her. If a bitch has several false pregnancies, spaying is the best solution, as she will go on having them after every season. It is an old wives' tale that mating will stop this, it will not. You will have to wait until the false pregnancy has passed before spaying, or the hormone will go on producing milk for some time.

7 *REARING A LITTER*

The first three weeks in the puppies' life should be the easiest for the breeder if the bitch is looking after them well and they are healthy.

A nursing mother needs four or five meals of high-protein food each day and access to enough water to produce plenty of milk. She will not want to leave the litter very much, especially in the first ten days, and will need taking out to relieve herself as she will not soil her bed and will not leave the litter voluntarily.

AFTER WHELPING

After the actual whelping is over, I change all the paper in the whelping box and replace with white paper. This is better than newspaper as the print does not make the pups grubby, and you never know what is in the printing ink. Wallpaper liner is good, as are computer sheets. Save a little pile somewhere clean in preparation for whelping time. You will have had to put dry paper in throughout the whelping as it is a messy and wet job.

Once she has settled with the pups, I am not too keen on changing the paper or bedding for the first few days as I think it helps with the bonding process. If everything is sterile and clean with no puppy smell, some bitches, especially first-timers, lose interest in the pups as they do not smell like theirs. So, never be too keen on wiping out the box with disinfectant and washing the bedding in bleach – you could be giving yourself trouble.

THE FIRST FEW DAYS

The first thirty-six hours of the puppies' lives is the most critical and, as their body systems are very immature, one of their main needs is warmth. This they get mainly from struggling up to the bitch's tummy and being tucked under her, but also from a heated pad. I carefully watch the litter, but do not

94

A beautifully reared litter – all these puppies went on to become Champions in the US.

handle them except when one seems to be lying away from its mother and siblings or needs a bit of guidance to the milk bar. Although all puppies are born blind and deaf, it never ceases to amaze me how they know where to go for food even in the first few minutes after birth.

I am not a breeder who weighs the pups either at birth or at any time during their infancy. I just know by looking at them – if they look plump and solid, they are alright.

As well as feeding her pups, Mother does another very important job by licking them, which makes them pass urine and faeces. You should not see any signs of puppy faeces in the whelping box as the bitch will eat it until the pups are about three weeks old. Some do it even longer than that, and I have had a bitch still cleaning up after one of her offspring when it was twelve months old, a disgusting habit but natural to her. I think one of the reasons that some dogs eat faeces in adult life is because they saw their dams doing it in the nest and copied them. Certainly, vets have come up with no good reason or remedy for it.

Healthy newborn puppies twitch and jerk a lot while they are lying in the nest between feeding times. They are also quiet except for the odd little cry when they fall off a teat or are crawling around looking for their mother.

SICKLY PUPS

A puppy who does not show signs of this activated sleep and lies still, or cries pitifully, is in trouble. Sometimes they can be helped by putting them to and holding them on a teat which you have squeezed some milk down. If the rest of the litter is very active, give the weaker one a chance by keeping the others away until it has had a good feed.

If the pup continues to cry that pitiful cry, like a wounded seagull, and is limp and cold when you pick it up with wrinkled skin and a purplish belly, your chances of rearing it are slim. Most importantly, if Mother ignores it, pushes it away and will not lick it even when you hold it to her, then you might as well give up on it. I firmly believe that this is the time when the bitch knows best and there is usually something

wrong with the pup which she can recognise but we cannot. We have all tried to hand-rear them, lost sleep feeding them every two hours and still had the heartbreak of losing them, so after thirty years of breeding I am guided by my instincts and the dams.

If a pup is crying a lot and upsetting the mother, then I take it away out of earshot and let it gently slip away. It is better to lose one out of a litter than for the bitch to get upset and not take care of the others. I believe that 25 per cent of pups born die in the first week, often for some reason we cannot see, but usually from being chilled, suckling poor milk, getting squashed or bad mothering.

FADING PUPPY SYNDROME

It cannot be called fading puppy syndrome if you only lose one. Rather, it is when one puppy after another starts crying pitifully, lies still and limply and has no interest in feeding. Mainly, this is caused by canine herpes virus and antibiotics do not seem to help. The cause is an infection in the vagina of the bitch and the sheath of the dog. The adults rarely show any signs so you will never know they have got it until you lose a litter. Before breeding either of them again they will need checking for infection and the appropriate antibiotics prescribed by your vet, but you can certainly say goodbye to most, if not all, of this litter.

ORPHAN PUPS

The worst thing that can happen to a breeder is to lose their bitch after whelping. This is much worse than losing the pups.

My first instinct after getting the pups warm is to look for a foster mother, as I believe pups never do as well as when they are looked after by a canine. Check with friends, not only in your own breed but any Toy breed, and let your vet know. The best thing would be a Peke bitch who had lost her litter or only had one pup. As Pekes never have big litters, you are not going to ask a foster mother to look after an extra five or six. It will depend entirely on whether the owner lets the bitch come to you or you take the pups to him or her. A bitch in her own home will be more inclined to accept strange pups than one who is changing environment at a fairly stressful time in her life. Peke mothers, I have found, are fairly placid and easy-going as long as they have a warm, comfortable whelping area and plenty of good food. It is not ideal to move them at this time, but I have had one of mine go to a perfect stranger and whelp and rear her litter until it was three weeks old before they could all return home, and she settled without any problems.

A number of my Pekes have been foster mothers, not only to Peke pups, and they have accepted the orphans without any problems. I introduce the new pups slowly one at a time after rubbing them around her vulva which is loaded with her scent. I stay with them all the time until I am sure she has accepted them and washed them properly and they have had a few feeds.

HAND-FEEDING

Hand-feeding is hard work, tiring and not always successful, so I suggest trying everywhere for a foster mother. But, until you find one or if you do not, the pups will need feeding and topping and tailing. For the first twelve hours a pup can survive on little feeds of just cooled boiled water with a little glucose added. If, after that, it is obvious you are going to have to do the whole job yourself, then the most important thing is to keep the pups warm. It does not matter how much or how good the supplement you give them is, if the pup is cold he will not be able to digest anything and will eventually die. Most pups, orphan or otherwise, die of cold, not hunger.

The easiest and most successful way to warm up a single pup, not so easy if you have a litter of three or four, is to put it close to your own body, i.e. in a pocket near skin, up your jumper, or, like I have done on occasions, down your bra! Once his temperature is back up to 94 degrees F (34.5 degrees C) and he is breathing normally and is having activated sleep, then you can start hand-feeding and have a good chance of rearing him.

Everyone has their own recipes for

puppy food, but I have had most success with a solution of 3:1 condensed milk and boiled water with added glucose and a couple of vitamin drops. This is a rich mixture, but it means you only have to feed every three hours during the first week and every four hours for the following ten days. A bitch's milk is very rich and high in protein and fat, and a weak alternative means the pups need more meals to give them enough nourishment.

Do not feed the solution cold, as this will just chill the pup's digestive system and cause tummy upsets which will hasten a pup's death.

BOTTLE-FEEDING

I make up a small amount of formula in a cup, warm it for ten seconds in the microwave and feed it, using a puppy-feeding bottle, when it reaches room temperature. I have used a dropper and syringe in the past, but found it gave the pups wind by conveying too much air. Also the puppies did not do any work by sucking, so I was the one who determined how much they ate. When they have to use their muscles to suck, it not only tells you when they have had enough so you can gauge the amount each pup is taking, but it keeps them more mobile and satisfies the nursing instinct. I think it makes them less inclined to develop chest problems, as they are swallowing the milk properly like they do when suckling from the dam instead of just having it put into

them and it not going right down to the stomach. The best way to ensure it goes straight into the stomach is by tube-feeding. Although I will explain the basics, I do think this is something you need to have demonstrated to you using a live puppy. It is quite worrying to do the first time, even with supervision.

TUBE-FEEDING

You need a piece of fine catheter tubing, the sort vets put down the throat when doing a Caesarian, but much finer. It needs to be at least twelve inches long. If you have any contacts with Bulldog breeders they will be able to obtain this for you as most Bulldog breeders are used to feeding this way, either because they have lost a dam or the dams have been clumsy and the pups have to be fed separately.

The main advantage of tube-feeding over bottle-feeding is that it is much less time-consuming and, when you have a whole litter to feed, this can mean a lot, especially during the night.

With your fine feeding tube you also need a 5-ml syringe. It goes without saying that these should be scrupulously clean and sterilised between each feed.

Holding the pup vertically in one hand, measure the tube against its body from mouth to last rib (which is approximately where the stomach is) and mark the tube with a marker pen or small piece of coloured tape. This will change as the puppy grows. Fill the syringe with the milk and attach the tube to the end, then push the plunger of the syringe gently until the milk gets to the end of the tube.

Whoever shows you how to feed this way will have their own way of holding the pup. You find the easiest way for you by trial and error. I hold the pup in my left hand by the head and gently feed the tube into the mouth, holding the tube about three inches from the end.

Put it straight towards the back of the throat and gently push it down, moving your fingers back along the tube until it stops or the mark is reached.

If it stops after the first inch or so, you have gone into the lungs, not the stomach, which means you must pull out gently and start again. When you are in the right place, hold the syringe straight up and depress the plunger steadily. When the milk is in, pull the tube out quickly.

Again, I will say that this method needs to be taught by someone experienced, not just by reading a book.

TOPPING AND TAILING

Whichever method you use to feed, if you have not got a bitch to clean the puppies you will have to do this yourself after every feed. For newborn pups, until they are four to five days old, I use dampened cotton wool (cotton) rubbing in circular motions around the lower part of their stomach, then I change to a dampened towel.

They will pass water very easily but it takes a lot longer for them to pass a motion and you need to be rubbing around the anus area. If the motions are loose or very yellow, you will have to alter your milk mixture as it is too rich. Pups should relieve themselves after every feed and at least three times a day. After about two weeks they will start doing it themselves. Mothers are washing pups up to 50 per cent of the day, so you should wipe their faces with a moist cotton wool ball and make sure they have fluffy bedding to snuggle into.

Make sure the pups do not start suckling one another. This often happens when tube-feeding as puppies need to use that nursing instinct. If they are doing it regularly it means they are hungry, so give more at each feed or feed more often.

Whether pups have a mother or not, do keep your eye on their toe nails and trim them back often. It is very painful for the bitch to have lots of little sharp nails scratching all the time. I was told years ago that, if you cut puppies' nails regularly very early on, then the quick will never grow long and so you will not run the risk of cutting the quicks and making them bleed when they are adult.

Usually, pups open their eyes at approximately ten days old without any problems but, if one eye looks a bit sticky, wipe it gently with cotton wool moistened in milk or warm water.

In relation to food, Pekingese are the Labradors of the Toy Group.

Photo: Keith Allison.

WEANING

Hand-reared pups can be weaned a little earlier than those feeding from a dam. There is no hard-and-fast age as to when to start weaning. If there are only one or two in the litter, the bitch will probably be happy to feed them to between three and four weeks, but any number over two need starting to wean at about three weeks old.

Everyone has their own special recipes to start pups eating. I, for one, am not keen on starting them on sloppy milky feeds and then changing to meat. Tiny digestive systems need as little upset as possible and, as they are going to spend the rest of their lives with meat not milk as a great part of their diet, I start them off on meat.

When I first came into the breed we were told to scrape small slivers of steak with a teaspoon and feed it by hand in a tiny ball. Thankfully, feeding has advanced a lot since then and there are many foods on the market especially made for puppies and which contain the correct amount of protein and vitamins.

Take the bitch out of the whelping area when you start weaning, otherwise the pups will get nothing. Likewise, do not feed dams their food in with the pups after their eyes have opened, as even the best of mothers can get possessive if she thinks a pup is coming too close to her bowl.

I use a flat plate to start with so that the pups can walk into it. It does not make any more work as the mother will come back and wash them clean. I use one of the quality canned puppy varieties, well mashed down with the back of a fork and made into a porridge with the addition of warm water. After a few feeds like this, I reduce the amount of water until the meat is just as it comes out of the tin. I also start using finely ground human consumption beef and hard-boiled egg well chopped up, for variety.

The bitch is still going in to the pups for short spells and I leave her in at night until the pups are about six weeks old. I start worming at this age as well. I know some breeders start much earlier, but I think that if the mother was properly wormed before mating, then this is early enough.

By the time the mother has stopped feeding the pups properly, they should be on five meals a day. Do be very careful about hygiene as the bitch will usually stop cleaning up after them once she sees you are providing the food regularly.

I do not give them milk to drink at all, but always leave a shallow bowl in the pen half-filled with fresh water which is changed a few times a day. As I feed an all-in-one complete feed during all their life, I start them at five weeks on moistened puppy biscuit mixed in with the meat and gradually increase the amount until they are getting more biscuit than meat for two meals a day. The other three meals will be meat, chicken or egg, and cheese which gives them extra protein until they are about four months old when they will be on three meals a day, but the majority of the food will be dry complete meal.

Remember, a Pekingese needs heavy body and bone, and this can only be made by good feeding when they are puppies. A heavy puppy should not just be a fat puppy; he should have solid little tree-trunk legs and the makings of a big ribcage.

I feed pups communally until they are about eight weeks of age, making sure that everyone gets around the plate, which is changed for a shallow bowl once I can see that everyone has got the idea. Sometimes pups are so keen to get their heads in that they overbalance and fall into the food head first, much to the surprise of their littermates! At eight weeks old they have a small bowl each, but are fed together in a puppy pen as I think competitive feeding encourages them all to eat up in case one of the siblings comes along to pinch theirs. Obviously, keep an eye on them at feeding times to make sure everyone is getting enough. I always think Pekes are the Labradors of the Toy world, as they will eat until they burst!

At ten weeks of age, this litter brother and sister show good physical development and share a healthy, inquisitive outlook.

Photo: Keith Allison.

During this time you should be decreasing the bitch's food so that she can get back into her normal adult feeding routine.

ASSESSING THE LITTER

Once the pups start wobbling about on their little fat legs, you will be able to see their personalities coming out. All pups are great time-wasters and it does not matter how many litters you have bred, you will still spend a lot of time just watching them play. Now is the time to handle them and get them used to strange noises. Mine are all brought up in the house, and the puppy pen is next to the television, the telephone rings all the time and they are within earshot of the dishwasher and other appliances which make noises day and night.

As I do not vaccinate until ten weeks, I do not let strangers in to handle them, but, in fine weather, they go out in a puppy pen near the front door and see anyone who calls.

This is when you can spot the shy ones and the ones who back off when anyone stops to talk to them through the mesh. Give these more of your time and attention and, usually, they will come out of themselves but, beware, if they still show signs after the vaccinations are finished at twelve weeks, let them go to nice pet homes, not be shown or bred from. It does not matter how lovely they are; if they have that shy streak matched with the typical stubborn Peke streak, they will let you down at a vital moment in the ring or pass it on if you breed from them.

8 *HEALTH CARE*

Pekingese are, in general, very healthy dogs, even the miniatures, and require very little veterinary assistance except in the cases of some bitches at whelping times.

The two main problems that are common to the breed are eye ulcers and slipped discs, and I will deal with these in more detail after going through the more common ailments.

GIVING MEDICATION

At some stage in your dog's life, you will be called upon to give either a tablet or medicine. It might only be a worming tablet or cough medicine, but it is important that you dispense it correctly and that the dog swallows it properly.

If the dog has not lost his appetite completely due to an illness, then the easiest way to give a tablet is hidden in a tidbit. I use something my Pekes do not normally have, so they know it is a treat and will tend to snatch it from you and swallow it greedily.

Push the tablet well into either a ball of best chopped (minced) beef or cream cheese, or whatever you know your dog really loves. Have another piece of goodie in your hand so he can see it. He will be so keen to get the second piece that he will swallow the piece with the tablet in without realising.

If he has no appetite, you will have to make sure the tablet is swallowed. Do this by opening the dog's mouth gently, putting the tablet at the back of the tongue and closing the mouth with one hand while gently stroking the throat with the other to make the dog swallow.

You must keep the mouth closed until you have felt the dog swallow, especially with Pekes as they are masters of tucking the tablet into their cheek and then spitting it out later!

The easiest way to give liquid medicine to a Peke, because of the flat face, is to administer it in a needleless syringe. The vet will let you have a few

Despite their small size and unique conformation, Pekingese are generally a healthy breed.

Photo: Keith Allison.

of these if you explain what you are using them for. Put the end of the syringe into the side of the mouth and squeeze a little bit at a time. Do not squirt it all in at once as the dog will spit it out.

TAKING THE TEMPERATURE

You take a dog's temperature by inserting the thermometer into the rectum. I use a child's thermometer with a digital display, which is readily available. Lubricate it so that it does not feel too rough, and insert it about 1.5 inches. It is easier if the dog is standing on a table while you do this; do not let him sit down, as the thermometer

might break. In an adult dog the normal temperature is 38.5 degrees C (101.3 degrees F). In small dogs, this is slightly higher, at 38.9 degrees C (102 degrees F). Modern thermometers will indicate when the actual temperature is reached, which is usually after two minutes. If you need to check your dog's pulse, the easiest place is on the femoral artery which is on the inside of the back leg where the thigh meets the abdomen.

EMERGENCY FIRST-AID

There are only a few things that you can do while getting in touch with your vet. Firstly, stay calm. If the dog senses you

104

are in a state of panic, then he will be more likely to go into shock, which will show itself as shivering, faint pulse, very pale gums and unresponsiveness. Keep him warm and still, and check his breathing. If he stops breathing, try mouth-to-nose respiration. Open his mouth, check for obstructions, pull his tongue forward and seal your mouth over his mouth and nose. Blow gently into his nose for five seconds, then stop for two seconds, then try again. Keep going until he breathes on his own or until you really feel there is no hope. You can also try heart massage, by placing your hand on the chest and pressing down very quickly up to one hundred times a minute. If you think your dog has eaten poison, try to find out what it was and get to the vet as quickly as possible. Do not try to make him sick as this wastes time and, for a number of poisons, is not the correct procedure.

If he is bleeding from a deep cut, apply pressure with a clean dressing held on firmly and get him to the vet where he will probably require stitches.

A-Z of COMMON AILMENTS

ANAL GLANDS
These are two glands situated at either side of the anus under the skin. They are there to help in passing motions and, if a dog is getting enough roughage in his diet, they cause no problems. If they become full and blocked, the dog will drag his bottom along the ground and run around trying to chew at his rear end. The glands then need emptying by your vet or another experienced person. Get them to show you how, but stand well clear because the fluid that emerges is usually evil-smelling and often comes out like a bullet from a gun. If the glands get really bad and become impacted and cause abscesses, your vet will recommend removing the anal glands.

BAD BREATH
Most Pekes seem to suffer from tartar on the teeth, especially the back ones, and this probably has a lot to do with the fact that judges do not open the mouth to check dentition and so breeders become lazy about cleaning teeth. I admit to being one of these, and end up trying to scale teeth which are usually only held together by tartar. Usually, they then drop out. I am against giving dogs anaesthetic just to clean teeth because there is still a risk of losing a Peke under an anaesthetic.

Really foul breath is one of the signs of stomatitis, which causes the gums to become inflamed and ulcers to appear on the cheeks and tongue. Such dogs have smelly grey saliva and the mouth is so sore they have difficulty eating. The infection can poison the whole body and often antibiotics do not work, so the only answer is to have all the teeth removed. Dogs can still eat as well with no teeth so long as they are not fed only on biscuit meal. A number of my oldies have gone for years with only three or four teeth in their mouths. Gingivitis is another condition which causes bad breath. This is usually caused by the build-up of tartar on the teeth which, in turn, can be caused by feeding soft food and not cleaning teeth.

There are very good canine toothpastes on the market, which not only clean the teeth but also release enzymes which help in keeping infections at bay.

One of the ways for feeling whether an infection is present is to check the two glands in the throat just below the back of the jaw. If these are swollen and feel like hard lumps, then you need to seek veterinary help and possibly antibiotics.

CANKER

This is the word used to describe the dirt in the ear which can be caused either by dirty wax or ear mites. The ear canal is made up of the long vertical segment at the beginning which angles abruptly and horizontally towards the skull. In Pekes, this is coupled with hairy hanging ear flaps which are the ideal warm, damp environment for infections to flourish.

Initially, the dog will scratch, shake his head or hold it to one side. The discharge will often be dark brown and smelly. Be very careful when cleaning out and do not go picking about with cotton wool (cotton) buds as this can

cause rupture of the eardrum. Clean out the ears once a week with cotton wool moistened with ear cleaning lotion (there are a number on the market), or surgical spirit. If the ears are dirty, then use a clean piece of cotton wool until nothing else comes out of the ear. If you cannot get them completely clean, it probably means an infection has set in or that there are ear mites present.

In either case, you need antibiotic drops from the vet who will put the ophthalmoscope, a magnified light, down the ear and will be able to see what the problem is. Mites show up as little grey things which are moving about all the time, causing the irritation the dog can feel. If a dog has scratched his ear furiously and for a long time, it can cause a haematoma, which is a blood-filled swelling on the ear flap. This will need draining surgically and should never be attempted by anyone other than a vet, because the amount of blood that can be produced is frightening.

Ear mites are contagious, so check all dogs that are in contact with the affected one and, if it is a severe case of mites, keep him separate until he is clear.

Never attempt to put water down the ear as this will cause many more problems.

CAR SICKNESS

This is not really a health problem, but can be very annoying and messy with

106

regard to the dog's coat. If you know you are going to take your Pekes out in the car, then do not feed them for at least two hours before. They are better going without a meal than having the contents of their stomach upped all over themselves, their bedding and the car seat.

If a dog has once been sick in the car, he will often remember this unpleasant experience and start drooling and dribbling the minute he gets in. Get Pekes used to the car when they are young puppies, with short journeys around the block. They are better if they start off in a travelling crate containing a towel or a fleecy bed so they do not slip about and become upset.

COLITIS

This is an inflammation of the colon (large bowel). Acute colitis can start very suddenly and not last very long. The physical (visible) signs are diarrhoea or motions with mucus or blood in them. It can be caused by bacteria getting into the colon and one of the best treatments it is to withdraw any fatty foods or ones that need a lot of digestion. Feed a bland diet with fibre for a few days, accompanied by natural yoghurt.

CONTAGIOUS DISEASES

When the puppies are born, they receive some natural protection against disease from their mother's milk through what are known as maternally derived antibodies (MDA). This protection is only temporary and will fade after a few weeks, so all puppies should be vaccinated before going to their new homes.

Puppies absorb MDA during the first few days of life from the colostrum in their mother's milk – so the more milk they get in the early days, the more immunity they have. The biggest puppy who drinks most is more protected than the smallest.

Vaccines work by containing a harmless form of the virus and stimulating the dog's natural defence mechanisms against that disease.

Puppies are never fully protected until they have had the second dose of the vaccine. This is because the high levels of MDA in some pups can sometimes knock out the first dose of vaccine as they are stronger, so that, by the time the levels of MDA wear off (between ten to twelve weeks of age), the pups can be completely unprotected. The second dose should be given on or after twelve weeks of age when MDA have usually disappeared.

Very occasionally, puppies can have an adverse reaction to the vaccination and appear listless or under the weather for a day or two. Even more rarely, they can get a 'blue eye' which is thought to be a reaction to the live hepatitis element of the vaccine.

DISTEMPER

Distemper used to be called hard pad in

the old days before vaccines were invented. Often carried by foxes as well as unvaccinated dogs, the disease is transmitted through moisture droplets and the incubation period can be as long as three weeks.

The symptoms include a wet cough, diarrhoea, high temperature, loss of appetite, sore eyes and a runny nose. Sometimes the dog's nose and foot pads can become hard and cracked; this is how the disease got its common name. In severe cases it can lead to fits, muscle spasms, paralysis and death.

HEPATITIS

This disease is caught by direct contact with infected urine, saliva or faeces. It can develop very rapidly, often within twenty-four hours. The symptoms include fever, abdominal pain, diarrhoea and vomiting and hepatitis can cause respiratory failure and death in a high number of cases. Survivors often become carriers for many months and can infect unvaccinated dogs without showing any signs themselves.

KENNEL COUGH

Despite its name, this infection is not only contracted in a kennel. It can be caught anywhere that dogs are brought together – dog shows, parks, training classes, popular walks, etc.

It is caused by a variety of infectious agents, including canine parainfluenza and the bordetella bacteria, and is passed on by inhaling contaminated airborne droplets or by direct contact with infected dogs. It is highly contagious and can spread rapidly where infected dogs are present.

The main symptom is a harsh dry cough without mucus, and one of the most typical signs is the dog retching as though he has something stuck in his throat.

Because it is so contagious, you should never take your dog where other dogs will be present and certainly never to a show without protection. It can last from a few days to a few weeks, depending on its severity.

LEPTOSPIROSIS

This occurs in two different forms. The first, carried by the urine of infected rats, is picked up by dogs swimming or drinking from canals and rivers where rats have been. I was told to always empty outside water bowls at night and upturn them in case rats came around and urinated in them. The symptoms of leptospirosis include high temperature, severe thirst, lethargy, vomiting and jaundice. It usually results in serious liver damage and is often fatal. This form of the disease can be transmitted to people.

The second form can be contracted in the first year of a dog's life from the infected urine of other dogs and the damage it causes usually only appears as the dog gets older, manifesting itself as kidney failure.

PARVOVIRUS

This is a fairly new canine disease, first appearing in the late 1970s. It has caused the death of thousands of dogs, especially puppies.

Parvovirus is easily passed from one dog to another through infected faeces. It can also be carried on the dog's hair and feet and can be walked in by humans. It is extremely difficult to eliminate and needs a particular type of disinfectant to kill the virus, which can be in bedding, grass runs and feeding utensils.

The most frightening thing about the disease is the speed with which it can affect dogs, especially pups. The symptoms include vomiting, high temperature and very smelly, bloody diarrhoea. Dogs rapidly dehydrate, although they seem to always be at the water bowl, and collapse is often followed by death, even if you get them to the vet at the onset of the symptoms. Puppies who survive are often left with a heart problem.

If dogs are going to walk or exercise where unvaccinated dogs are present, they should always be up to date with their boosters, although there is a strong feeling that boosters need not be given every year, but perhaps every three years. Be guided by your vet on this, but always ensure your puppies have their full course of vaccinations.

RABIES

This is a viral disease that is transmissible to all mammals, including man. It is spread mainly by the fox in mainland Europe, and by the raccoon in the United States. As the disease changes the sufferer's character, an affected animal may well wander into populated areas that it would normally avoid, and become a serious threat to both domestic animals and to man.

Those countries in which rabies is endemic have far less fear of the disease than those, such as the UK, which are clear of it. Nevertheless, its serious implications for man have led to rabies vaccinations for pets being compulsory in some countries, such as the US, while others, like the UK, have traditionally relied upon quarantine to control the disease. Much improved vaccines are now available and, increasingly, there is a move towards a combination of vaccination and blood-testing rather than lengthy isolation for animals imported into a rabies-free area.

CYSTS

Interdigital cysts occur mainly on the tops of the pads or between the toes, and are usually noticed because the dog spends a lot of time licking and chewing his feet.

Poultices made up of a pad soaked in hot water will help to burst the cyst and draw the poison out. You might have to do this a few times before it empties, then apply antiseptic cream or powder. If this does not work, the vet will lance it like a boil. If a dog starts licking his feet, do have a good inspection as the sooner you start treating the problem, the quicker it will be healed and the less discomfort your dog will feel.

Sebaceous cysts appear on the body, usually in animals with greasy skin. They usually empty after gentle squeezing; often the pus comes out like a white worm. Wash them with warm water and apply antiseptic cream. If sebaceous cysts keep recurring the vet can cauterise them. They are not a problem to the dog, but often you catch the comb in them when grooming and cause them to bleed.

CYSTITIS

This is an infection of the urinary system. Dogs and bitches can suffer from this but bitches seem to be more affected.

It is usually caused by a bacterial infection which comes from the genital tract. Another cause is the retention of urine either by an obstruction, like bladder stones or a growth, or sometimes even by a house-clean animal not being allowed to go out and relieve itself.

Some show bitches get it from going

THE FEMALE LOWER URINARY TRACT.

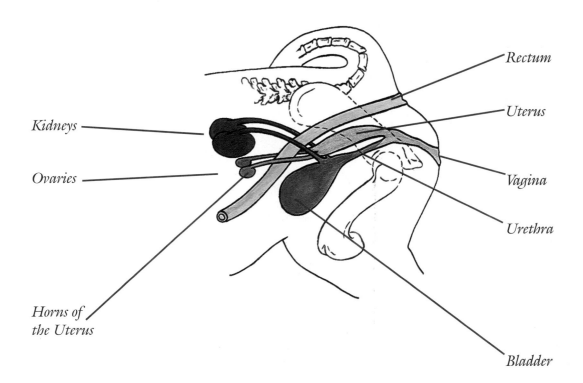

Rectum

Uterus

Vagina

Urethra

Bladder

Kidneys

Ovaries

Horns of the Uterus

on long car journeys and not relieving themselves until they get home.

You can usually tell when a bitch has cystitis as she makes numerous attempts to pass water, squatting and straining for a long time and then only producing a small amount which often has blood in it, smells foul and is thick liquid.

Veterinary help should be sought sooner rather than later, as cystitis is more difficult to cure as time goes on. Your vet might want a sample of urine so he can determine which antibiotic to use on the bacteria. This is not always easy to get but, if your bitch will relieve herself on newspaper, then put a glossy magazine down, as the urine does not soak through so quickly and you will be able to pour it into a container.

DIARRHOEA

Dogs get diarrhoea from a number of causes, overexcitement or nervousness, a change of diet or water, intestinal parasites such as worms, viral and bacterial infections, or eating something upsetting or even poisonous.

Withhold food for 24 hours, but make sure the dog drinks plenty of water to stop dehydration. Glucose can be added to the water, and it is better if the water is boiled and left to cool. Often, arrowroot mixed in with a white bland diet when he starts to eat again will clear up the last symptoms.

Kaolin mixture or Immodium can be given for up to three days. If the diarrhoea is not clear by then or if there

was blood in it, you should let the vet see the animal as it may be a symptom of something more serious.

ECLAMPSIA

This condition is caused by lowered levels of calcium in the blood and usually occurs soon after whelping, especially if it is a large litter, otherwise about three weeks after whelping.

It does not matter how much calcium you have given a bitch during pregnancy, she can still have eclampsia. The body can only absorb so much calcium and excess is passed through. The signs are that the bitch becomes hyperactive; she is restless, hides in a corner, starts rejecting the pups, sometimes salivates and becomes wild-eyed. If ignored and not treated, she becomes very excitable and twitches a lot. Often this is accompanied by a lot of yelping or even showing the teeth as in aggression.

A bitch can collapse and go into a coma very rapidly, so you must get to the vet as quickly as possible. This is a real emergency and she needs intravenous injections of calcium and glucose. These injections bring a bitch round very quickly with no apparent ill effects.

If the condition has been brought on by a large litter, I would advise supplementary feeding to help the bitch, as well as early weaning.

Also make sure the bitch has a diet high in calcium from eggs, milk and cheese. I also feed a calcium tablet daily after whelping until mother has finished feeding the pups.

I do not feed calcium supplements while a bitch is in whelp, as there is some suggestion that over-supplementation can increase the chance of a bitch suffering from eclampsia.

HEATSTROKE

If you have taken the precautionary measures mentioned in the chapter on showing, open-mesh pens, ice packs under the dog and wet towels over the pen, possibly a fan (battery operated if you are away from an electrical outlet), then, hopefully, you will never experience this. But, due to the brachycephalic head (shortened muzzle or flat face), it is more difficult for a Peke to cool himself down by panting, as his nasal airways are very short.

Dogs do not have sweat glands on their bodies like humans and can only reduce their body heat through their mouths by panting. As Pekes have thick heavy coats, they do feel the heat more than most breeds and so it goes without saying that they should never be left outside in direct sunshine without being able to get into the shade. Never should they be left in a stationary car in warm weather; cars can become like ovens very quickly and leaving the windows open will not cause enough draught to prevent what can be very serious and often fatal overheating.

The signs of heatstroke are rapid loud breathing, bright red mucous membranes and a wild expression with the eyes very bulging. The rectal temperature will be very high and affected dogs will become unsteady on their feet before collapsing.

You have got to lower the temperature very quickly because excessive breathing and the shock will put a great strain on the heart and can lead to death.

If heatstroke happens at home, the fastest remedy is to open the freezer door and hold the dog gently in the cold blast. Keep talking to him all the time because, if he is in shock and his vital organs are starting to close down, hearing is the last thing to go and listening to your voice talking to him calmly and gently can give him the strength to carry on. Obviously, do not leave him alone or close the freezer door. Do not let him stand or lie down on the floor of the freezer without a towel to protect his feet from the frost.

If you do not have access to a freezer, put him in a bath or sink of cold water up to his neck. Do not have the water ice-cold to start with, as icy water can cause the blood vessels to constrict and slow down evaporation, which can cause the temperature to rise even further. Add ice cubes as he begins to relax or put him, while still wet, in front of a fan. Once the dog has become calmer and more relaxed, then keep him quiet and away from other dogs and gently pat him dry so that he does not get cold.

Phone the vet and tell him what you have done, but do not be in a hurry to put him in the car and take into the surgery, especially on a hot day, unless your car is air-conditioned.

Remember, prevention is better than cure, so be extra-vigilant on hot days, especially if you have a black dog, as black coats seemed to hold the heat more than other colours.

HERNIA
There are two main types of hernia. The umbilical is usually associated with puppies and occurs when a lump of fat appears on the abdomen, where the umbilical cord has been, because the umbilical ring has not fully closed.

Hernias can be inherited or made. A bitch with a hernia will often produce pups with the same, however careful you are at whelping time. If the hernia is large, it is best to have it surgically treated and not breed from a bitch with this problem. Sometimes the tissue surrounding the umbilical area may be weak and the dam pulling on the cord can cause the hernia. Often these are very small and get proportionately smaller as the puppy grows, causing no problems, so it is best to leave them alone.

Inguinal hernias consist of a swelling in either side of the groin and are usually seen in adults. They are caused by a protrusion of the abdominal organs through the inguinal canal in the groin. These are best treated by the vet before they cause problems such as strangulation, when they have to be treated as an emergency before the blood supply gets cut off.

PARASITES

INTERNAL PARASITES
There are a number of different types of internal parasitic worms such as the heartworm, hookworm, threadworms and lungworms and, most commonly, roundworms and tapeworms.

ROUNDWORMS (TOXICARA CANIS)
Everyone has their own worming regime and a lot depends on the medication used. There are syrups on the market which can be given to pups from two weeks of age. Pups pick up roundworms from their dam while in the womb, so it is very important that bitches are wormed before mating. Apart from seeing the worms, which are passed in faeces, the other signs to watch out for are a distended stomach and a dull lifeless coat.

Whether you see any signs or not, regular worming should be part of canine health care.

TAPEWORMS
These are connected to fleas, as this is commonly how the egg is passed to the dog, so it is very important that you check for and eradicate fleas, as well as using the correct wormer for

tapeworms, which is different to the roundworm medication.

Signs of tapeworms are small segments like grains of rice which appear around the anus. These segments have passed through from the intestine and carry the eggs, which hatch out. When the dog licks that area they are transported back into the intestine and start reproducing all over again.

HEARTWORM

This parasite lives in the heart (actually inside the right-hand chamber of the heart) and in the major artery to the lungs. Heartworms can cause significant problems in the dog, the symptoms being easily confused with other heart diseases. Heartworm tends to be found in specific areas, usually rural communities, where mosquitoes (the intermediate host) are found. Modern wormers are very effective and should be used routinely in areas where heartworm is endemic.

EXTERNAL PARASITES
FLEAS

There are so many products on the market to spray or bath dogs that fleas should never be much of a problem. When a dog starts scratching, look well into the coat right down to the skin. If you do not see the flea itself, you will see the droppings which look like black pepper. If these are put on wet paper they turn browny-red which is a sure indication of fleas.

As well as spraying the dog, and the best places are behind the ears, along the spine and under the chest, you must spray the beds. Wash all blankets and bedding and vacuum well into the corners and edges of carpets. Only a very small percentage of fleas live on the dog; the rest are in the house.

There are some products on the market that the dog takes orally, but I am against giving anything internally if there is another way of treating a problem. Spraying or shampooing will probably need to be done more than once, as fleas can live away from the host for a long time.

LICE, TICKS AND MANGE MITES

Hopefully you will never see any of these parasites in your Peke, but, if a dog is scratching and no other cause can be found, it may be that you have some of these visitors. It will take an examination of a skin scraping by the vet to determine just what the problem is, but they are fairly easily treated once the problem is pinpointed.

PATELLA

The patella is the correct name for the kneecap in the dog. Many small breeds, including Pekingese are prone to patellar luxation, which is sometimes called 'slipping patella'.

The bone of the kneecap sits in a groove and is held in place by the patellar ligament. In small breeds, the groove is often too shallow and so the bone can slide out sideways. Sometimes you can actually push the patella out of place to one side or another. When it is out of place, the dog cannot straighten his leg and will tend to hold the affected leg up for several steps until it pops back in again.

Many dogs live with this condition without seeming to suffer any discomfort. If it starts in a puppy without any reason, i.e. an accident, then it is congenital and should be deal with surgically before serious deformity sets in.

PYOMETRA

This is a disease of the bitch's reproductive system. It can be quite common and, if not treated in time, can be fatal. The uterus fills with fluid which usually contains bacteria.

It more often occurs in bitches of five or over who have never had a litter, but it can happen in younger bitches, usually about a month after they have been in season.

There are two types, open and closed. In the open type, the signs are more visible as there is usually a thick red-brown, very smelly discharge from the vulva. The closed type is harder to detect as there is no discharge, but it is usually more severe. Poison from the vulva is absorbed into the bloodstream and gives the signs which indicate problems. These are usually excessive thirst, swollen stomach, excessive urination, and sometimes vomiting. If

untreated, pyometra causes shock and often death.

See the vet without delay, as the bitch will usually need an emergency operation to remove the uterus. If you catch the condition early, you may be able to treat her with drugs and save having to have her spayed, although there is a high risk of it recurring after the next season.

There are drugs which can control a bitch's season and reduce the chances of pyometra. Your vet will advise you about these and any risks involved.

SKIN PROBLEMS

If a Peke gets a skin allergy, you must treat it quickly, not only to relieve the dog's discomfort but to save the coat. Once they get an itch, they can scratch and chew at their coat until they get bald patches.

The most usual causes of skin problems are flea allergies which need treating in two ways, both on the dog and in all the bedding. Often, after spraying the dog, they still continue to bite at the skin. In this case, use tea tree oil lotion which is very soothing and antiseptic. If that fails, an antihistamine injection usually does the trick. An allergic reaction to something they have eaten will either make Pekes sick or give them diarrhoea. In that case, starve the dog for twenty-four hours but make sure they have plenty of water, as diarrhoea is very dehydrating. After twenty-four hours, only feed white meat like chicken and fish mixed with rice. I am a great believer in feeding hard-boiled egg the day after a fast or whenever Pekes have runny motions for no apparent reason, as the egg helps to bind them up.

In the old days, a block of sulphur was often added to the drinking water to help cool the blood because this causes the dog to scratch at his coat. Good old calamine lotion put on the affected area often helps in mild cases.

SOFT PALATE

The soft palate is situated behind the upper molar teeth and extends back into the throat. It is a muscle whose function is to close off the nasal cavity when a dog is eating, so that food is directed down the gullet.

It is particularly long in a dog and can, especially in short-faced (brachycephalic) breeds, cause a temporary obstruction of the airways into the nose when a dog becomes excited or overheated. The dog will open his mouth and breathe hard and loudly because the air catching at the back of the throat causes the flap of skin at the back to move.

Encourage the dog to relax and quieten down, and the muscle will relax into its correct position. A dog with this fault should never be placed in a position of stress such as whelping, or in the heat, as the consequences could be fatal.

EYE CONDITIONS

Pekes tend to have more problems with eyes than most other breeds, due to their shape and placement. Exophthalmic is the medical term for a Peke's prominent eye. Very rarely nowadays do you see the very bulging eyes and, therefore, there are fewer problems in the breed than there were. Most present-day eye problems are caused by knocks and rubbing the eye to get rid of irritations.

ROUTINE CARE

Eyes should be checked every day and wiped over with dampened cotton wool (cotton). Do make sure the hair from the wrinkle does not grow into the eye and, if it is long, it would be better to snip it shorter with round-ended scissors. If this is too frightening a task to contemplate, smooth Vaseline on to the hair of the wrinkle and press it away from the eye. One of the first signs of eye trouble is that the dog starts to blink a lot or rub his eye either with his paw or by rubbing his head against something like the carpet or even the mesh sides of his pen, which will quickly accelerate the problem.

Often the first sign an owner will see is the pale blue clouding which is called 'blue eye'. This can sometimes be caused by a draught, so make sure affected dogs are not sitting outside in the wind.

FOREIGN BODIES

A good thing to clean the eye with, and hopefully flood out any foreign bodies, is a sterile saline solution such as contact lens wearers use. Then apply an ophthalmic ointment or drops. I prefer the ointment, as I think drops wash out too easily. Do not let the top of the ointment tube make contact with the eye; apply the ointment by lifting up the top eyelid and squeezing it in and, when the dog blinks, the ointment will go down on to the cornea. Apply the ointment as often as possible. I sometimes do it up to eight times a day. I always have a tube of veterinary dispensed eye ointment in the house. If you know the cause of the injury (such as a protruding piece of something sharp or a rose thorn) get rid of it. The more injuries an eye gets, the weaker it becomes and the more sight it loses. Often an injury is caused by a nail from a companion's paw catching the eye when playing, so keep your eye on any future rough-and-tumble behaviour.

If there is no improvement after three to four days, let the vet have a look. He will put a drop of coloured liquid in, which will stain the eye and show up the ulcer which might need more assistance – such as stitching the eyelids together to give the ulcer a better chance of healing.

ENTROPION

Some eyelid problems can cause corneal abrasions, such as entropion which is where the lower eyelid turns in towards the eyeball and the eyelashes rub and irritate the eye. This needs veterinary help and usually an operation, and certainly the affected animal should never be bred from.

There are other eye conditions such as distichiasis which is a double row of lashes, usually on the upper lid. I have also heard of puppies with hair growing from the centre of the eyeball. For these conditions, veterinary advice should be sought as soon as possible.

PROLAPSE

If eyes are looked at every day and wiped out regularly, there should be no problems. It is an old wives' tale that, if you pick Pekes up and shake them, their eyes will pop out. Complete nonsense! But it is possible that you may, once in a lifetime, experience a prolapse of the eye. This usually happens because of a fight when another dog catches the skin at the side of the eye. Because of the large eye and shallow eye socket, the eyeball pops out.

This is very frightening to see, but you must stay calm and move quickly if you want to save the eye and any hope of full vision. Pull the eyelids wide apart and press the eyeball with the ball of your hand to get it back in quickly before it starts swelling. You really need two people to do this, but speed is of the essence as, once the eyeball has swollen, you will not get it back in. If this does not work, immediately phone

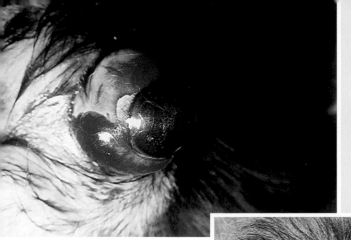

A prolapsed eye. Note the swelling which makes it impossible to push the eye back manually.   Photo: K. Fraser.

Minutes after arriving at the surgery, the dog has already been anaesthetised. All the swelling is behind the eye.

Photo: K. Fraser.

The eyelids is being drawn together before stitching. The dog is anaesthetised.

Photo: K. Fraser.

the vet, cover the eye with a wet, clean dressing and get to the surgery as quickly as possible. Sometimes vets are able to save the eye, but the dog has to be sedated and the eyelids stitched together for ten days.

I have had three dogs during thirty years of breeding that have lost an eye because the blood vessels had swollen the stem behind the eye and it was impossible to get back into the socket. All of these three have lived to old age without being upset with only one eye, and have lived with a group of dogs

118

without anyone noticing any difference or causing any trouble.

On the plus side, I once had a very famous Champion who had a little scrap with another stud dog and his eye popped out. Luckily, I was in the room but I was on my own. To keep the eyeball moist while I tried to push it in, I held his head under the cold water tap. I managed it after using quite a bit of force and getting the dog and myself completely soaked with water. He went on to win another ten CCs and nobody was any the wiser.

BACK PROBLEMS

Back problems in Pekingese seem to be getting more common. This may be because of longer backs coming into the breed, combined with heavy bodies and short legs, but there are more cases of disc problems, some even leading to paralysis.

The first signs are that the dog seems quiet and certainly will not want to play. He will usually lie in one position and, when picked up, as well as crying out with pain, he will tense his body, especially his stomach, and hold himself very rigid. Often this is mistaken for a stomach problem since the stomach is very hard as the dog tenses his abdominal muscles to prevent any movement of the spine.

What has usually happened is that the intervertebral discs, which are located between the bones of the spinal column, have slipped out from their normal position as the pads of cartilage have weakened and lost their elasticity. The disc then touches the spinal column and, depending on where it is pressing, affects the severity of the pain and where the problem manifests itself.

Some studies have shown that this is a degenerative disease and not caused by injury to the back. Some people think that letting Pekes run up and down stairs can cause disc problems, but mine do that every day without any ill effects. I personally feel it is a weakness in certain lines which means that some dogs are more predisposed to suffer than others. Often you will find littermates having the problem, even if their upbringing has been different. The higher up in the spine, such as the neck, the worse the problem is, and, in the most severe cases, all four legs will be paralysed.

You will need the help of your vet, but do not be too quick to rush into surgery. Initially, start with cage rest, keeping your Peke confined in a small pen, so he cannot move around. Only take him out to relieve himself.

He will probably be given a steroid injection and then a course of medication which will combine steroids and analgesics. These will shrink the swelling in and around the spinal cord and ease the pain and inflammation. This treatment should last at least ten days, even in minor cases, as the use of steroids can make you and the dog think they are cured before they actually are. If they get back into normal routine too early, then it can cause a worse problem and could end in surgery.

If there is no real sign of improvement, then the vet will take X-rays which will show up the exact location of the slipped disc. Often, these have to be more exact than a normal X-ray so the dog might have to go to a specialist for a myelograph, in which a dye is injected into the space around the spinal cord to show up exactly which disc is causing the problem. If a specialist deals with these problems, then he may also perform a MRI (magnetic resonance imaging) or a CT scan (computerised tomography). At this stage, the vet would be almost certainly contemplating surgery. This entails removal of bone to expose and relieve the pressure on the spine and removal of the offending disc.

This operation relieves the pain at once but the dog is often very poorly post operatively and Pekes often have heart failure just after surgery or as they are coming round. Those who pull through need very careful aftercare.

Even just using cage rest and medication, you must remember that there is a weakness in the back and, even if it never occurred in the same spot again, Pekes should not be allowed to do anything too strenuous.

I find that Pekes who have had back problems are more careful themselves and tend to pace themselves more, like the intelligent dogs they are.

NURSING THE SICK AND OLD

A dog that is ill requires similar nursing to that of a human. Warmth, quiet, comfort and plenty of TLC (tender loving care).

Pekingese are quite brave and will not show signs of illness until they are pretty poorly – and usually by then they need expert veterinary care.

Try to keep the patient away from any other dogs, preferably in another room, because he will often try to join in with what is going on before he is fit. I once had a young Peke dog with a broken jaw who wanted to inspect every bitch that passed him, in case she had come into season while he had been at the surgery! Although Pekes are usually pretty clean in the house, put newspaper down if your dog is not able to get outside, otherwise you will have bladder problems added to ill health. If an older Peke has had an eye operation, make sure there are no sharp objects he can bump into while he is adjusting to only seeing from one eye.

Cosset your Peke by giving smaller meals more often, especially if he has had stomach problems or a bitch has had stitches from a Caesarian or spaying. If a Peke haas had teeth out, make the first few meals soft and palatable, as their gums will be sore.

Elderly Pekingese often end up with very few teeth, but it does not seem to affect their appetite. I do not change diet for my oldies, but I make sure they have longer to eat their own food before the younger ones come to inspect the bowls for any leftovers. All of my dogs have their daily diet split into two meals a day, as I think this is better for a small stomach. Sometimes the oldies, who do not want to eat much at one time, appreciate having lunch as well as breakfast and dinner.

Pekes usually live to a ripe old age compared to many other breeds. The oldest I knew was twenty-one. My oldest lived to nineteen, and the majority last until fourteen or fifteen. Of course, like people, Pekes sleep longer as they get older and certain things start letting them down, like their hearing and sight.

Make sure the older dog has a comfortable bed with dry blankets, as, not only will he spend more time in it but he will become arthritic, and it will be harder to move about.

Slight coughing can often mean heart problems, so let the vet check your dog over. As well as heart medication, an older Peke may also need diuretics as their kidneys might not be working as well.

Check ears and eyes regularly, as an older dog's immune system is not as good as when he was younger and there is more chance of infections.

THE FINAL DECISION

However long dogs live, it is never long enough and the time will come when you have to say goodbye. I think all owners pray that their beloved pet will die in his sleep, in his own basket, before the quality of life has gone. But this does not always happen, and you have to make that terrible decision for your Peke. Sometimes we are selfish and want to keep them with us for a bit longer, not wanting to say goodbye to a beloved pet who has been part of our lives for so long. Whether your Peke is a Champion, or a dog that did not rise to such heights in the show ring, or a bitch that stayed at home and produced the winners, or one that did none of those things but was a constant companion, the hurt is just the same.

Euthanasia is the one thing we can do for our canine family that we cannot do for others. It is never done lightly, but, if a dog is suffering with no prospect of improvement, if he has no pleasure left in life and every move is a struggle, surely it is a kindness to relieve all this? Nowadays, vets very rarely make house calls and, if they do, they can be very expensive, but it is better if your companion can end his days in his own surroundings. Wherever you have it done, do stay with him or her until the end so that they can hear your voice and know that the person they loved for so long was still with them. They will not know it is the end and the actual injection is a painless overdose of anaesthetic.

Do not be afraid of showing your grief; no animal lover will think less of you. I cry every time it happens and, after thirty years in Pekingese, it has happened a lot of times. It never gets any easier, but try to remember the good times. If this was your only dog, do get another one. Your last companion would not want you to be lonely and you are not trying to replace him; nothing will. Every dog has his or her own unique personality with lots of love to give.

If you have once had a Pekingese, you will not want to contemplate life without one. You never forget past ones and if, like me, you have them buried in the garden, there is always some reminder; a clump of daffodils, a bush, a cherry tree in blossom. However, there is nothing like looking into those deep pools of eyes, smelling that distinctive faint powdery smell, listening to them snoring, or watching that confident unique walk, tail up over its back, to convey the feeling of being owned by a Pekingese!

9 THE PEKINGESE IN BRITAIN

The Second World War was a watershed for the Pekingese in Britain, as it was for many breeds. Food shortages meant that most of the kennels had to be disbanded, and with the peace came new opportunities for new names. These are the kennels that have made their mark in the years since.

YUSEN

The Yusen kennel was quick to make its mark after the Second World War. Yusen Yu-Toi, bred by Sally Higgs, won the first open show organised by the Pekingese Club and went on to become the first postwar Champion.

Yusen Yu Chuo was the sire of the famous Puffball Of Chungking, owned by Mabel Cliff (later Fryer), who in turn sired numerous winners. The most notable of these was Ch. Ku Chi Of Caversham, bred by Elfreda Evans out of an Alderbourne dam, who went on to win 30 CCs plus Best in Show at Crufts in 1950. A red dog weighing only 7½ lbs (3.4 kgs), he was a great showman and an influential sire. His progeny included Ch. Caversham Ku Ku Of Yam, winner of a record 40 CCs. Ku Ku won seven Best In Shows at all–breed Championship Shows between 1954 and 1957 and is still regarded by many to be the model of the breed. He sired nine English Champions, including first Champions for Chintoi, Drakehurst and Copplestone.

Other descendents were to include Ch. Ku Chik Ku Of Loofoo, who won the Dog CC three years on the run at Crufts including the Toy Group in 1958, and Ch. Goofus Le Grisbie, BOB at Crufts in 1964 and later an American and Canadian Champion.

KYRATOWN

Owner Hindley Taylor bought his first brood bitch when he was twelve and had the first postwar Champion bitch in Lovely Maid Of Kyratown. By 1970 he had won 312 CCs since the war.

Pictured (left to right): Ch. Beau Of Kyratown with Hindley Taylor, Ch. Beaupres Belle with Fiona Mirylees, Miss Pinkcoat and Mr Pinkcoat Copplestone with Yve Bentinck – all bred in the same litter by Ruby Charlton.

COPPLESTONE
The Copplestones of Mrs Bentinck were known all over the world. Two of her best were miniature brother and sister Mr Pinkcoat and Miss Pinkcoat (Bonny and Clyde). Mr Pinkcoat became an Irish Champion and they were both exported to America to join the kennels of Betty Shoemaker.

CHANGTE
Pauline Bull started the Changte Kennel in the 1930s, and remained a major influence on the breed for the next four decades. Although there were many Changte Champions and the stud dogs sired Champions for many other kennels, the most famous dog was Ch. Chuffy's Charm Of Changte. He was the result of seventeen generations of the Changte strain, as Mrs Bull rarely used an outside line, and was top Stud Dog between 1973 and 1975. He won 17 CCs and, like all the Changtes, was instantly recognisable.

CHERANGANI
Cherangani was another kennel that was easily recognisable in the ring. The best-known Champion, owned and bred by Mrs Stewart, was Ch. Cherangani Chips, who was a sire of Champions.

JAMESTOWN
Jean Eisenman firmly established her own type in the Sixties. She based her line on Caversham but used a lot of in-breeding and line-breeding, which quickly established an easily recognisable type of dog: shapely bodies of great substance, large open faces with beautiful, large, dark, lustrous eyes. They were usually a clear red with black muzzles, as opposed to the full black masks of the darker reds and greys in the ring at that time. This in turn meant that those large eyes held your attention from the minute you looked at them.

A number of Jamestown Champions made their mark in the ring. The first homebred Champion was Suzie Wong Of Jamestown, who won her first CC from Miss Ashton Cross and her third from Miss de Pledge. She in turn produced the great Ch. Fu Yong Of Jamestown, who was a stud force on both sides of the Atlantic. The dog most people think of when you mention Jamestown is Ch. Yu Yang, a grandson of Fu Yong out of Ch. Jinette (who also went to America). He sired many Champions, including Ch. Chyanchy Ah Yang Of Jamestown, who was owned by the Sawyers and sired six Champions.

Eng. Am. Ch. Fu Yong Of Jamestown: A stud force on both sides of the Atlantic.

Ch. Yu Yang Of Jamestown, pictured at six months of age.

Ch. Chyanchy Ah Yang Of Jamestown: Son of Ch. Yu Yang Of Jamestown.

Ch. Drakehurst Hsu-Yang Of Jamestown: Son of Ch. Yu Yang Of Jamestown.

Many kennels used the Jamestown lines to great advantage. Dorothy Dearn's first Champion, Dorodea Yu Song, was a daughter of Ch. Yu Yang and her second, Petite Beurre, was a grand-daughter. This kennel had some excellent bitch Champions and the black male Champion Dorodea Dark Rhythm sired a number of winners.

RALSHAM

Barbara and Carole Lashmar's Ralsham kennel was another to succeed with the Jamestown bloodline. Their Champion bitch Ch. Ralshams Lovely Lady was sired by Ch. Chyanchy Ah Yang and later sold to America.

The kennel's first Champion back in the Fifties was Ralshams Donna Beauty and her near namesake, Ch. Ralshams

Eng. Am. Ch. Ralshams Lovely Lady: Exported to the USA.

Ch. Belknap Bravo: Toy Group winner.

Ch. Ralshams Lady Ku Donna: Crufts CC winner 1988.   Photo: Hartley.

Ch. Singlewell Little Else, owned by May Young, sired by Ch. Singlewell Wee Sedso.

Lady Ku Donna, won the CC at Crufts in 1988.

Lovely Lady's sister produced Ch. Ralshams Humdinger in her first litter and her second, to Laparata Celestial Star, produced the dam of English and New Zealand Ch. Ralshams Aristocrat, who was the grandsire of Lady Ku Donna.

BELKNAP

Jamestown breeding was also the basis for the Belknaps of Antonia Horn. Ch. Suzie Wong was the first Champion, but she bred many more herself, including the two black and tans Nero and Scarteena.

Ch. Eldorado was a Best in Show winner at an all breed Championship

Ch. Adlungs My My My: sired by Ch. Shiarita Cassidy. *Photo: Fall.*

Show, and she had group wins with Bravo and Pocket Peke. She never campaigned the dogs to multiple wins (Pocket Peke was her biggest winner with 10 CCs) as she usually had something else waiting in the wings.

The only Champion she ever sold was Ch. Belknap Kalafrana Caspar, a son of Ch. Shiarita Cassidy out of Ch. Belknap April Shower, who was a daughter of El Dorado. Caspar went to Mrs Maynard in America, where he won his American title and sired many Champions.

Mrs Horn also bred the litter brother and sister, Champions Bravo and Blush.

Mrs Horn judged a record entry of Pekes at Crufts Centenary Show in 1991. She had 267 dogs entered and her BOB, Ch. Pemyn Sheer Elegance At Tenling, went on to Reserve in the Toy Group. She died six months later and her remaining Pekes went to live with her great friend May Young at the Adlung kennel.

May's first Peke Champion was Singlewell Little Else, who started her show career with her breeder Pam Edmond and gained her title with May Young. Using local sire Belknap Bravo she bred the litter brother and sister, Champions Adlungs Rah Rah and Sweet Charity.

ST AUBREY ELSDON
In 1967 Nigel Aubrey-Jones, R. William Taylor and the St Aubrey Elsdon Kennel moved from Canada to England. They were a force to be reckoned with in the

Ch. St Aubrey Pekehuis Petula: Top winning bitch with 35 CCs. *Photo: Fall.*

seven years before they returned to North America. The exquisite Ch. St Aubrey Fairy Ku Of Craigfoss won 17 CCs. She was a grand-daughter of Ch. Mr Redcoat Of Kanghe. Their next Champion was a daughter of Mr Redcoat, Ch. St Aubrey Pekehuis Honeydew, bred by Mrs Partridge of the Pekehuis kennel, who later bred the top winning bitch Pekehuis Petula.

LAPARATA
After their return to Canada, Messrs Jones and Taylor made a trip to Britain and saw a nine-month-old puppy bred by Mrs Snook of the Laparata prefix. Although this male was a very reluctant

showman, Nigel Aubrey-Jones was impressed by him and managed to buy him. He went on to become Ch. St Aubrey Laparata Dragon, one of the most influential sires in North America.

Mrs Snook bred and exhibited a number of dogs to their titles, including Laparata Regal Star, who was sired by one of the most prepotent sires of the last twenty years, Ch. Jay Trump Of Sunsalve. Her first champion was Ch. Laparata Celestial Star, whose sire Etive Copplestone Pu Zin Julier (who went back to Caversham Ku Ku Of Yam) was a Champion on both sides of the Atlantic.

KHANGE
Ch. Mr Redcoat Of Kanghe, owned

and bred by Queenie Mould, was an influential sire in the Sixties. A number of his winning progeny carried his lovely bright red colour, including Ch. Genderlee Sargent Pepper Of Palaquin, who was a grandson of Ch. Cherangani Chips. Mr Redcoat was also the sire of Ch. Beau Of Kyratown (later exported to America) and his litter sister Ch. Beaupres Belle.

BEAUPRES
Beupres Belle was one of a number of Champions for Betty Mirylees and daughter Fiona. She gained her title aged seven and at eight won BIS at Darlington Championship Show.

Mrs Mirylees had five daughters and her eldest, Dawn, initially handled many

Ch. Beaupres Belle: This bitch became a Champion at seven years old, and won BIS all breeds at the age of eight.   Photo: Fall

Ch. Lady Gay Of Beaupres: Winner of 13 CCs and BOB Crufts 1978.   Photo: Fall.

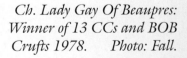

of the winners, including Ch. Beaupres Lovely Star Of Grimstoy, who was bred by Mrs Williamson out of her Ch. Ku Nanette Of Grimstoy, a daughter of Ch. Ku Chik Ku Of Loofoo.

Later Fiona took over in the ring and handled Ch. Samotha Gay Lad Of Beaupres, and his progeny, the brother and sister Beaupres Likely Lad Of Patrona and Ch. Lady Gay Of Beaupres, and many others, to their titles.

Many Beaupres went abroad, especially to America, and became Champions in their new lands.

Fiona judged Crufts in 1983, when her bitch CC was Ch. Teijon Shy Won and her Dog CC and BOB Ch. Some Man Of Lotusgrange.

KYBOURNE
Joy Montrose based her stock on the Changtes and soon had success. Her first Champion, Kybourne Crystal Coral Of Changte, also produced her second Ch. Kybourne Coral Prince. Crystal Coral won the Bitch CC at Crufts in 1971 when Yu Yang won the Dog CC and Best of Breed.

MICKLEE
The first Peke to go Reserve BIS at Crufts was Ch. Micklee Roc's Ru Ago in 1985. The breed judge on that day was Dorothy Dearn and Ru Ago went on to win 26 CCs. The Micklee kennel is owned by Joyce and Jack Mitchell and their first Champion was Simon Of Belrosa. There have been 19 Champions bearing the Micklee prefix, and although the Mitchells no longer show, the prefix has been put in joint ownership with Stuart and Andrea Livesey who have campaigned two males to their titles.

OAKMERE
Oakmere's Olive Clay is a great lover of parti-colours, although none of her Champions have been this colour. But Oakmere Dolly Daydream Of Upcot, who was not only a parti but a sleeve as well, was one of the most well-known Pekes of her time due to her fascinating character. The first Oakmere Champion was Sandiacre, who was made up in 1964, followed by a daughter of Simon Of Belrosa, Oakmere The Countess, in 1974.

Ch. Oakmere The Countess.

Ch. Toydom Sunshen Chu T'Sun: The sire of Pam Edmond's first Champion, Ch. Singlewell Sun Chu.

SINGLEWELL

One of the oldest prefixes still showing and in the hands of its original owner is Singlewell. The prefix was registered in 1947. Pam Edmond and her mother, Mildred Wolfe, based the line on Caversham and Alderbourne. The majority of the Singlewell Champions have been bitches, although the first, Sun Chu, in 1966, was a male. The amazing Singlewell T'sai Magic, who not only won 15 CCs but produced four British Champions and four overseas Champions in four litters, was surely the most famous.

Magic's most influential son was Ch. Singlewell Magic Ruler, who was sired by Ch. Micklee Roc's Ruago and is the sire of Champions, including Tomdor Randolph Of Singlewell, his brother Tomdor Rule's Son Of Singlewell, and the black Ch. Singlewell Cilla.

When Magic was mated to Ch. Jay Trump Of Sunsalve, she produced Ch. Singlewell Magic Charm. Two years later, the mating was repeated and produced Singlewell Sensation and Singlewell Celebration, who went on to become a French Champion.

Jay Trump has already produced a Champion for the Singlewell kennel in Singlewell Jay's Dream, out of Donelco Sheeza Dream, who was Magic's dam. Jay was a great grandson of Ch. Singlewell Wee Sedso going back through Sungarth Kanga Of Toydom, who appears behind many of the present-day winning Toydoms. Sedso

Ch. Singlewell Magic Ruler: Sire of many Champions.

Ch. Singlewell Sensation and French Ch. Singlewell Celebration: Litter sisters pictured at ten months, daughters of Ch. Jay Trump Of Sunsalve.   Photo: Chambers.

Ch. Singlewell Harlequin.

Ch. Singlewell Jay's Dream: Sired by Ch. Jay Trump Of Sunsalve.

was a grandson of Ch. Mr Redcoat Of Kanghe and Ch. Singlewell Sun Chu.

The latest Singlewell, Ch. Harlequin, goes back to Toydom and is a parti-colour like his sire Ch. Delwin Another T'zee.

LOTUSGRANGE

Another long-established kennel still showing and winning are the Lotusgranges of May Robertshaw. She registered her prefix in 1954 and soon had a small kennel of winning stock that were known from the early days for superb bodies and bone. The kennel was based initially on Caversham and the first Champion, Jina Of Lotusgrange, was a Ch. Ku Jin Of Caversham grand-daughter. She was BOB at Crufts in 1963 when Ch. Sandiacre Of Oakmere, the first Champion of Olive Clay, won the Dog CC. The judge was Miss Cynthia Ashton Cross.

Later May added some Jamestown blood and from a mating to Ch. Yu Yang produced Ch. Lotusgrange Shorona. Her next Champion Maybelle was by Ch. Samotha Gay Lad Of Beaupres. Litter sister Gaybelle died tragically in an accident, otherwise they would have been Champion litter sisters.

In 1980 a male puppy came back to Lotusgrange from a mating, sired by Lotusgrange Jamesman, who was heavily line-bred. Ch. Some Man Of Lotusgrange gained his title at two years of age and went on to win nine CCs. He was BOB at Crufts in 1983, when Ch. Teijon Shy Won won the Bitch CC, and soon established himself as notable sire, producing Ch. Lotusgrange Again The Same, out of a daughter of Ch. L Shorona.

His most influential son was probably Ch. Pemyn Some Guy, who in turn was the sire of Ch. Pekehuis Sir Guy, winner of 37 CCs and top-winning Peke male of the last twenty-five years.

Ch. Only A Wish Of Lotusgrange Of Cynling was bred by May but sold to Cynthia Sterling and became the first Champion for this new exhibitor in 1973. She was sired by Fu Yong Of Lotusgrange, who went on to be a Dutch Champion for the Eastcourt Kennel of the Oosterhofs.

Ch. Pemyn Some Guy.   *Photo: Fall.*

Ch. Pekehuis Sir Guy: Winner of 37 CCs, BOB Crufts 1987, BIS Birmingham Championship Show 1989, Top Pekingese 1987-1989.   *Photo: Fall.*

Ch. Tenling Golden Arrow Of Pekehuis: Top Dog 1993, 1994, 1995, 1996. Photo: Hartley.

Some Man also sired Ch. Bryndora Of Lotusgrange, who went back on her dam's side to Singlewell T'sai Magic and Singlewell Wee Sedso.

Again The Same sired Ch. Acirema Some Girl Of Lotusgrange. She and Ch. Play It Again Of Lotusgrange both became Champions in 1993. Some Girl, when mated to Ch. Tenling Golden Arrow Of Pekehuis, produced Ch. Lotusgrange Arrow Express, who won his third CC at Crufts in 1996 under judge Terry Nethercott of the Sunsalves. Play It Again sired the latest Lotusgrange, Ch. Play Time, who gained her title in 1998.

A total of ten Lotusgranges have been shown to their title by May, who judged Crufts in 1987. Her BOB was Ch. Pekehuis Sir Guy.

TOYDOM

This famous kennel name, which started in the Twenties, is still going strong. It was begun by Mrs Alex Williams, known for her lovely dogs and large hats, and is now carried on in the South by her daughter Vandy and partner Adele Summers.

In the early days the Toydoms were shown alongside the Alderbournes, Kyratowns and Cavershams. Staff and food were cheap, and as many as 100 dogs were kept at one time. At the outbreak of the Second World War, the Toydoms had more Champions than any other Peke kennel.

One of the great winners of the

Thirties was Ch. Toydom Manzee followed by his son Ch. Toydom Manzee Tu. The first Toydom Champion after the war was Ch. Toydom Jewel Of Elfann, who was sired by the great Puffball Of Chungking. In 1953 came Ch. Toydom T'szee, a fawn and white parti-colour, who won 14 CCs. He was BOB at Crufts in 1956. By the mid Sixties Mrs Williams had just about stopped showing and by the time she died in 1973, the Toydom strain had almost died out.

Toydom Trump Card: Sire of Ch. Jay Trump Of Sunsalve.

However Vandy and partner Adele Summers decided to start the kennel up again and began looking around for stock. Their most important buy in those early days was Sungarth Kanga, from Beryl Prior. He became the cornerstone of the new kennel.

Sired by Ch. Singlewell Wee Sedso out of a Yu Yang daughter, he won three reserve CCs. But he more than proved his worth as a stud dog, siring their first Champion, Ch. Toydom Erotica. I awarded their first CC in 1979.

Their next good buy was Dorothello Gay Loretta Wong from the Sunsalve kennel. She was mated to Kanga and produced Toydom Trump Card and Toydom No Secrets.

Trump Card was mated to a Sunsalve bitch and produced Ch. Jay Trump Of Sunsalve, who went on to be such a dominant stud.

The next Toydom Champion was from No Secrets, who was mated to Ch. Belknap Eldorado and produced the

Adele Summers with Toy Group winner Ch. Toydom Modesty Forbids.

133

Ch. Toydom Modesty Permits.

Ch. Toydom Quite Outrageous.

Ch. Toydom Back With a Vengeance.

Ch. Delwin A Little Bit Special: The first Champion for Grace Godwin.

lovely Ch. Toydom Modesty Forbids, winner of three CCs in 1981. In the same year they campaigned Ch. Toydom A Touch Of Class to his title. He was by Trump Card out of a daughter of Kanga. In 1982 he won a strong Open Dog class at Crufts under Pauline Bull and went on to win Dog CC and BOB. Again, I gave this dog his first CC.

Modesty Forbids was a difficult dog to show – being typical Peke – but he won the Toy Group the day he won his first CC. It was as a sire that he really made his name, producing Ch. Belknap Bravo and Ch. Belknap Blush out of Ch. Belknap April Shower (an Eldorado daughter). He also sired Ch. Toydom Modesty Permits for the home kennel out of a Trump Card daughter.

Kanga also sired another Champion in Toydom Dutch Courage, who was out of his grand-daughter, as a number of Toydoms began to make their presence felt abroad. Many were Kanga offspring.

In the late Eighties came the sister and brother Ch. Toydom The Drama Queen, who sadly died in whelp, and Ch. Toydom's Quite Outrageous. He went on to sire Ch. Toydom Back With A Vengence, who in turn sired Ch. Singlewell In Vogue With Toydom, so there is still a strong male line of Toydom Champions.

Grace Godwin and the Delwins have now joined forces with the Toydoms and her latest champion, the parti-colour Delwin Another Ts'zee, who was sired by Ch. Toydom's Quite Outrageous, has already proved himself at stud. He is the sire of Ch. Singlewell Harlequin. Grace's first Champion, Delwin A Little Bit Special, had produced four litters before gaining her title.

PEKEHUIS

The kennel was started in 1948 by Mrs Ethel Partridge with a Caversham bitch and the first Champion was the black Ch. Chartaway Yung T'sun, who gained his title in 1960. Two years later the kennel bred its first Champion Mingshang Pekehuis Bi-Jou Shah. She went BIS all breeds at Southampton Championship Show in 1965, the first Pekingese bitch to achieve this honour.

The biggest winner from this kennel was Ch. Pekehuis Petula, who won 35 CCs and is still the bitch record holder. She was sired by Honourable Mr Twee Of Kanghe, who was a son of Ch. Mr Redcoat Of Kanghe. Mr Redcoat had earlier sired Pekehuis Honeydew, who was sold to Nigel Aubrey-Jones and Bill Taylor and became a Champion for the St Aubrey prefix. Petula produced a

Ch. Pemyn Sheer Elegance: BOB Crufts Centenary Show 1991.

Ch. Pekehuis Pure Gold Of Tenling: Top sire 1995 and 1996.   *Photo: Hartley.*

Ch. Joleth Octarine Alchemy.

Champion bitch, Ch. Pekehuis Petal, when mated to Ch. St Aubrey Carnival Music Of Eastfield.

Winifred Mee, who had worked at the kennel since 1958, took over the prefix on Mrs Partridge's death in 1985. She bred her first Champion, Ch. Pemyn Some Guy, in partnership with Joan Cross. He was sired by Ch. Some Man Of Lotusgrange out of a bitch who went back to Ch. Chero Queen and Ch. Micklee Romeo.

Some Guy was mated to a Ch. Pekehuis Petal grand-daughter and produced the 21 CC-winner Ch. Pekehuis Sir Guy, who went BIS at Birmingham National in 1989.

Some Guy's dam Regina had two sisters and, when these were mated to Sir Guy, he produced Ch Pemyn Sheer Elegance Of Tenling for Winifred in her new partnership with Mr and Mrs Tennant, and Ch. Pemyn Morning Star for owner Kathy Kinsey. Sheer Elegance was BOB at Crufts in 1991 and second in the Toy Group. The Dog CC that year was Ch. Tomdor Randolph Of Singlewell.

While in Canada, Winifred saw Am. Can. Ch. Rodari Orient Express and persuaded owner/breeder Barbara Melles to let him come to England. He won the Reserve CC at his first show and became a Champion within the year. He was a son of Am. Can. Ch. Knolland Red Rover, who was a top sire for Michael Hill in Canada. Orient Express, when mated to a grand-daughter of Sir Guy, produced Ch. Tenling Golden Arrow Of Pekehuis, who was top-winning Peke male in 1993, 1995 and 1996.

Golden Arrow sired Ch. Pekehuis Pure Gold Of Tenling for the home kennel as well as Ch. Lotusgrange Arrow Express for May Robertshaw and Ch. Joleth Octarine Alchemy for Mrs Gilson.

KETTLEMERE

Another kennel with a long pedigree, it was founded by Lilian Shipley and is now carried on by her daughter Joyce.

The two names that spring to mind are the first Kettlemere Champion Margo, who won 19 CCs, and her daughter Ch. Matilda, who won her title in the United States and in Bermuda. The kennel has always concentrated on its bitches and Joyce carried this tradition on by campaigning Lien Prunella Of Kettlemere to her title after her mother's death. I gave this bitch her first CC when she was still a puppy.

In the mid eighties Joyce acquired a bitch descended in direct line from Ch. Margo and who was also a grand-daughter of both Ch. Shiarita Cassidy and Ch. Prunella. From this line she bred and campaigned her first Champion in her own right. This was the black Ch. Kettlemere Midnight Dancer, who was a daughter of Ch. Dorodea Black Rhythm (a great-grandson of Ch. Yu Yang). Dancer has

Ch. Kettlemere Midnight Dancer.

already produced a Champion daughter in Kettlemere Midnight Storm when mated to Golden Arrow. She produced Kettlemere Midnight Madness, winner of two CCs and six reserves, when mated to Ch. Yakee Dame's Desire Of Shiarita. Midnight Madness had her show career curtailed due to a marked eye, but she is producing winning stock such as Midnight Melody and Midnight Magic.

PASCAN
Judith Risbey is noted for producing good bitches with her Pascan kennel.

Her first Champion was Pascan Perfect Lady who was a grand-daughter of English and American Champion Etive Copplestone Pu Zin Julier and great-grand-daughter of Yu Yang.

The next Pascan Champion was Pascan Pursuit Of Love, sired by Ch. Nowai Harvey Moon. The repeat mating produced Ch. Pascan Poetry In Motion who, when mated to Ch. Nowai Alexander Moon, produced the winning dog puppy Pascan Puccini – a combination of two strong lines. She was unlucky not to get her third CC with Pascan Putting On The Ritz, who was a grandson of English and Irish Champion Shiarita Peter Pan.

Ch. Pascan Perfect Lady.

Ch. Pascan Poetry In Motion.

NOWAI

The Nowai kennel of Brenda and Alan Sheppard produced their first Champion Harvey Moon in the early nineties, and he won his first CC at ten-and-a-half months old from Jack Mitchell (Micklee). He went on to win 26 CCs and was still being placed in Toy Groups at five years old. He also sired champion stock.

Alan always showed the dogs while Brenda did the grooming but, after Alan's untimely death, Brenda took over the handling and campaigned Nowai Alexander Moon (a Harvey son) to his title, and Nowai Sidney Moon, a Harvey grandson.

SHIHGO

Harvey Moon's sire, Ch. Tomdor Randolph Of Singlewell, also sired Ch. Shihgo Idle Gossip, who sired a number of Champions for the Shihgo kennel and others. He became a Champion in 1995 and in 1996 was top stud dog.

He really clicked for the home kennel when mated to Tilouet Silver Queen At Shihgo, a double grand-daughter of Ch. Shiarita Cassidy. This produced Ch. Shihgo Idle Dreams, who won her first CC at Crufts in 1996 under Terry Nethercott and became Top Peke and Top Toy Dog in 1997 (making her breeders Top Breeders in 1996). She also won the CC at Crufts in 1997 under Geoffrey Davies, who himself owned two Shihgo bitches which he made into Champions. Both Juicy Tit Bit and Gossip Column were campaigned together during 1996.

Four years earlier he campaigned two half brothers, Star Attraction and Too Close For Comfort. The latter won the Toy Group at Crufts in 1993 after winning the CC and BOB from Nigel Aubrey-Jones.

In 1989 he campaigned a male that he had bred himself to his title – Ch.

Ch. Nowai Harvey Moon: Sire of Ch. Nowai Alexander Moon, Ch. Pascan Pursuit Of Love and Ch. Pascan Poetry In Motion.

Ch. Shih-Go Idle Dreams: Top Pekingese and Top Toy Dog in 1997

Ch. St Sanja Too Close For Comfort: Toy Group winner, Crufts 1993.

Genderlee Jin's Jester, a grandson of Ch. Shiarita Cassidy. That same year the other Cassidy sons, both bred by Bert Easdon and Phillip Martin of the Yakee prefix, were winning CCs.

YAKEE

Bert Easdon's Yakee kennel is based in Scotland – but the many miles clocked up on the Championship Show circuit have never deterred this prolific winner. Ch. Yakee For Your Eyes Only began 1989 by winning the Toy Group and Reserve Best in Show at Crufts, only the second time a Peke had achieved such an honour. He had started his show career in 1987 with his litter sister, Ch. Yakee Gentlemen Prefer, who had won three CCs before she was twelve months old. One month later she won her fourth and qualifying CC and became a full Champion. Sadly she died suddenly before she was able to breed on.

For Your Eyes Only went on to win 22 CCs, many Groups and Best in Show at all breed Championship Shows, and he really made his mark as a sire, too. As he was heavily line-bred to Cassidy he clicked with a number of lines. In 1989 Yakee The Charmer, another Cassidy son – this time out of their first Champion Yakee Patent Pending – was Top Sire.

Bert has so far campaigned 14 Champions, from Yakee Patent Pending to the latest, Sweet Caroline. These have included Charm School Deb, her son Got Wot It Takes (who won the CC at

Ch. Yakee For Your Eyes Only: Reserve BIS Crufts 1989, winner of 22 CCs.

Ch. Yakee Patent Pending.

Crufts twice and was second in the group there in 1992), The Hoi Polloi and her daughter Good Vibrations, who won the CC at Crufts 1993. Among the others were Slightly Saucy, Your Place Or Mine, All Eyes On Me (another Charm School Deb offspring), Crazy For You (a Good Vibrations daughter) and Angel Eyes (another Group winner).

Ch. Brentoy Jacinta At Yakee, bred by the Charltons, was Ch. Jay Trump's last Champion daughter, and Ch. St Sanja Grand Finale At Yakee was from the last litter of For Your Eyes Only. As well as being a multiple CC winner, he has won Groups and BIS all breeds. His litter brother St Sanja Here I Go Again became a Champion handled by Winifred Mee.

Ch. Yakee Gentlemen Prefer: Litter sister to Ch. Yakee For Your Eyes Only.

Ch. Yakee Sweet Caroline.
Photo: Carol Ann Johnson.

Ch. Yakee All Eyes On Me.

Photo: Carol Ann Johnson.

SHIARITA

The prefix was registered in 1966 by myself and husband Paul, and our first Champion, Beckee, was born in 1968, a daughter of Ribocco Of Loofoo. She won her first CC in 1970 under Fiona Mirylees, who coincidentally awarded a first CC to our second Champion, Shiarita Ladybird.

Meeting up with Jean Eisenman (Jamestown) at shows, I realised that I wanted the large dark eyes and beautifully cushioned faces of the Jamestown dogs, as well as the bodies and bone we already had, so the breeding plans took a complete about-turn and we started using Yu Yang.

The turning point came when a dog belonging to Jean I had long admired was given to me as a Christmas present. Sungarth Echo Of Jamestown was not only a Yu Yang grandson, but brother to Kanga. He had a fierce temper but was the mirror image of his grandsire – that

lovely, bright apricot colour and those glorious dark pools of eyes.

One of the bitches from Jean, Jamestown Yu Darling Of Lotusgrange, a Yu Yang daughter, when mated to Echo, produced our first male Champion Shiarita Lingsam. The following year we mated Ladybird to Sam's Legacy and produced Ch. Shiarita Hello Dolly, our next Champion. Lingsam and Dolly, both tightly line-bred to Jamestown with an outcross line for deep pigmentation and sound rears, could not fail and this was proved correct in their first mating.

Only one puppy was born on that day, January 8th 1977, but what an impression he was to make on the breed...Shiarita Cassidy. He went to his first show at seven months old and won his class. In fact he won all his puppy classes and, on the day he was nine months old, he won the CC and BIS at the British Peke under Lyd Kinnersley.

Ch. Beckee Of Shiarita: The first Champion for this kennel, made up in 1970.

Sungarth Echo Of Jamestown.

Shiarita Cassidy, pictured at seven months of age.

Eng. Ir. Ch. Shiarita Peter Pan: Winner of 17 CCs.

He won his second CC at ten months and his third under Heather Dearn (Dorodea). He won 22 CCs in all plus many Groups and Reserve BIS all breeds. He retired at three-and-a-half years old after winning the CC and BIS at the British Pekingese Diamond Jubilee Championship Show, topping an entry of 208 dogs under Queenie Mould (Kanghe).

Cassidy had a limited stud career, but in his few outside matings he produced Champions for a number of people.

Apart from those already mentioned there was Penbi My Fair Lady, Belknap Kalafrana Casper (who won his title in America as well), and Shiarita Fort Lauderdale (who was also an Irish Champion). He and Ch. Shiarita Peter Pan, another Irish Champion, were the only two in the country for many years and the only two dual Champions in the same kennel. Peter Pan won 17 CCs and went one better than his sire by winning BIS all breeds at a general Championship Show. His dam was by

Monarch, mated to a Yu Yang daughter.

He sired Ch. Shiarita San Francisco, whose mother was a Cassidy daughter and Legacy grand-daughter. He was the first Shiarita Champion to be sold and he went to friends in Holland who made him a Dutch and World Champion.

Diamond Lil was the result of a father to daughter mating, her dam being Peter Pan's litter sister, and was two-and-a-half years old before she went in the ring. Lil won 20 CCs, the first at only her third show, and ended the year as Top Peke. She also won Groups and Reserve BIS all breeds.

Ch. Shiarita Bob by Dazzler was the result of a grand-daughter to a

Ch. Shiarita Bobby Dazzler: BOB Crufts 1998.   *Photo: Pearce.*

Ch. Yakee Dame's Desire Of Shiarita: Sire of Ch. Shiarita Emperor Roscoe.

The only Pekingese kennel to have had a Champion sire and five Champion offspring all living under one roof, in 1989.
Pictured (left to right): Ch. Shiarita Cassidy, Ch. Yakee Dame's Desire Of Shiarita, Eng. Ir. Shiarita Peter Pan, Ch. Shiarita Bobby Dazzler, Ch. Shiarita Diamond Lil and Eng. Ir. Ch. Shiarita Fort Lauderdale.

grandfather mating and his daughter, Ch. Shiarita Bobbie's Girl, is out of a Cassidy daughter. Not only was Cassidy top Peke for the three years he was shown, but he was top sire in 1979, 1980, 1981, 1985, 1989 and Top Toy Sire in 1989. He sired thirteen English Champions and many overseas.

Ch. Yakee Dame's Desire Of Shiarita is a repeat of the mating which produced For Your Eyes Only and Gentlemen Prefer, and was the last Champion son of Cassidy. I was very lucky to be able to obtain him from Bert Easdon as he was already a winning puppy.

Dame's Desire was the sire of Ch. Guzmac Be My Desire and Ch. Shiarita Emperor Roscoe, winner of eight CCs in this country. Roscoe then went to America where he was campaigned to his American and Canadian titles. His new owner, John Shaw, then sent him to Holland to the Oosterhofs and he soon won his Dutch title, too. He then rejoined his owner in Hong Kong and became a Hong Kong Champion as well as an Asian Champion – the only English-bred Peke to gain all these titles.

Before he left England, he sired a Champion for the Lees in Ch. Frampton Gift Of Love. He sired a Dutch Champion for the Oosterhofs and an American Champion bred by them. Another half-brother from Holland has now come to start his show career in Britain and there is a Champion son in Hong Kong.

The latest Champion at Shiarita is another Dame's Desire son, Shiarita Billy Fury. He is our fifteenth Champion.

OTHER WINNING KENNELS

Gary Thomas from Wales is a young man who has had some great wins in his short time in the breed. His famous young male Ch. Jonsville Daytime Lover won three Best in Shows at general Championship Shows in 1988 to make him Top Peke that year and Top Dog. I gave him his third CC and he went on to win 17 CCs and four Toy Groups. He was sold to Holland in 1990.

Gary's first Champion, Jonsville Magic Touch, was sired by Paragold Lady's Wot A Boy Of Bramblefields, who was a Ch. Chyanchy Ah Yang grandson and was owned by a young couple from Wales, Phil and Jackie Jones. He was also the grandsire of Daytime Lover.

In 1988 Phil and Jackie made up another grandchild of Wot A Boy in Ch. Bramblefields Berangari, their first Champion. She was quickly followed by their second – Ch. Bramblefields Organza, who won her first CC under myself and quickly gained her title. She won the CC and BOB at Crufts in 1990 under Joyce Mitchell.

Another couple from Wales that had some lovely bitches in the Seventies were Nancy and Bert Kerkin, who based their Wei Sing Prai kennels on Caversham and Jamestown. Ch. Pixie Of Wei Sing Prai and her daughter Ch.

Ch. Jonsville Daytime Lover: Three times BIS at all breed Championship Shows, and winner of 17 CCs.

Photo: Fall.

Pollyanna, who won twelve CCs, were two of their outstanding bitches. Pixie was the grandmother of Ch. Sunsalve Queen Bee Of Lejervis, who was owned by Mrs Rolfe Hazell but bred by Terry Nethercott and sired by one of the top studs of the Seventies and Eighties, Ch. Jay Trump Of Sunsalve.

This amazing little dog was used at stud very heavily and, although he did not produce a similar type, he was able to produce winners and Champions for many kennels. He was a grandson of Sungarth Kanga Of Toydom and so went back to Jamestown on his sire's side, but his dam was a bit of a mixture.

Ch. Sunsalve My Love.

Sungarth Hi-Jack, brother to Hi-Jinks.

145

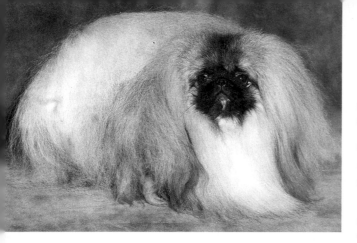

Ch. Jay Trump Of Sunsalve: Top sire 1982-1986.

He was a very glamorous fawn with a black face and was always beautifully presented by Terry.

He won seven CCs but it was as a sire that he really made his mark, siring Champions such as Cambaluc Songbird Of Toydom, who was owned by Sue Mannering. Josto Royal Flush and Josto Madam Gaye At Sunsalve were both bred by Mrs Stokoe, but Gaye was owned by Terry, as was Royal Flush's daughter Ch. Josto Airs 'N' Graces.

Eileen Newman had Jay's son Ch. Rosayleen Casino Royale, who sired Champions including St Sanja The Thought Of You, Tirakau Royal Replica and Rosayleen The Gaffer At Sunsalve (who also became an American Champion).

Ch. Sunsalve My Love was another Champion for Terry and partner Eddie Hurdle, who leaves the showing to Terry. My Love had an interesting pedigree as her dam, Forget Me Not, was litter sister to Ch. Sungarth Camellia and her grandmother, Carole Of Carona, was also the grandmother of their first Champion Sungarth Hi-Jinks Of Sunsalve (bred by Beryl Prior). Hi Jinks litter brother Hi-Jack was the grandsire of Jonsville Magic Touch.

Carole, when mated to Yu Yang, produced Sungarth Anchusa, who was the dam of Sunsalve Echo Of Jamestown and Sunsalve Kanga Of Toydom. Her litter sister Sunsalve Aconite was the dam of Hi-Jinks.

Mrs Snook had a Champion by Jay in

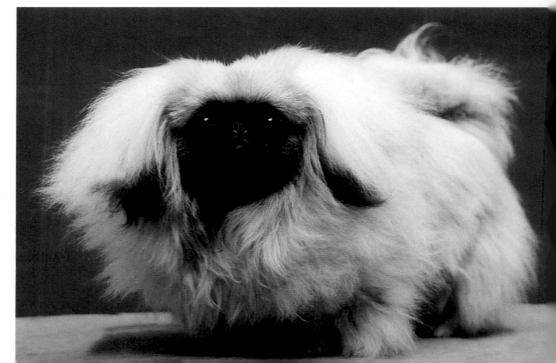

Ch. Guzmac Jin's Solitaire.

Photo: Dalton

Ch. Trimbar Mee-Mee For Siyasu.

Ch. Guzmac Be My Desire.
Photo: Leigh.

Ch. Laparata Regal Star. The Toydoms also produced Champions Toydom The Drama Queen and Toydom Quite Outrageous from the same litter when mating his half-sister to Jay.

He was Top Sire in the breed from 1982 to 1986 and produced countless numbers of overseas Champions.

Marion and Gordon Fearn are another kennel that have had some success with different colours. Their Ch. Fearnvale Potters Viola was a parti-colour and they have won CCs with blacks.

The Bartrim family won the CC at Crufts with Ch. Trimbar Fanny (a For Your Eyes Only daughter) out of their Ch. Trimbar Yvette. Most of their Champions have been a combination of Micklee and Shiarita, such as Ch. Trimbar Oberon, Trimbar Sweet Fanny Adams, and Trimbar Gef-Ree.

Trimbar Fanny's litter sister, Trimbar Mee-Mee for Siyasu, became a Champion in 1993 for owners Sue Woolway and Dave Wilkins and went on to win ten CCs.

Ch. Frampton Gift Of Love. Photo: Trafford.   *Dratsum Midshipman Hendrix.*

Ch. Lynbank Honeysuckle Rose:
Sired by Shiarita Bobby Shafto.

Another fancier breeding and showing winning stock is Marjorie MacDonald, whose Ch. Guzmac Jin's Solitaire was a daughter of Ch. Genderlee Jin's Jester. Ch. Guzmac Be My Desire was a son of Ch. Yakee Dame's Desire Of Shiarita, and his son, Guzmac All My Desire, is already a CC winner.

Marjorie's daughter, Lynette Shaw, has also been successful in the breed with Ch. Shawmar Ravishing Ruby and Ch. Shawmar Saucy Secret.

Obviously I cannot mention everyone in the breed during the thirty years that I have been involved. The one thing we all have in common is the love for this magnificent, independent creature who gives us so much love and devotion in return.

We must all remember that we are only custodians of the breed, carrying on where others have left off and hopefully leaving it better for those who come after us.

10 THE PEKINGESE IN NORTH AMERICA

BY ANTHONY ROSATO

From the time the Pekingese was first introduced to North America, and a small Peke, owned by Mrs George Thomas and known simply as Pekin was first shown in Philadelphia in 1901, the breed has endeared itself to a number of prominent exhibitors. The Pekingese has come to enjoy a lion's share of the spotlight in all breed dog show competition, particularly during the last half of the 20th century.

In America, the breed has had a number of stars over the years, including three illustrious Pekes who have attained the highest honour in North American dogdom, that being, of course, the honour of winning Best in Show at the prestigious Westminster Kennel Club show at Madison Square Garden. The first and most famous Peke to win this honour, Ch. Chik T'Sun of Caversham, who until 1980 held the exalted long-time record of most AKC all breed Bests In Show for any breed, retired with 126 BIS to his credit.

EARLY FANCIERS
Some of the early fanciers to influence the success and popularity of the Pekingese during the first half of the century include Mrs Jane Austin, whose Ch. Che Le Matson's Catawba was one of the first multiple all breed Best in Show winners, handled by Ruth Sayres. However, the very first all breed BIS

Int. Ch. Fu Yong Of Jamestown:
One of the top sires of the 1960s.

went BIS in 1955, at Westchester KC, handled by Nigel Aubrey-Jones, with an entry of 2,000 dogs, quite a huge entry at the time. This great win catapulted the breed into a new star status, giving it an unprecedented respectability in the eyes of the judging community, and thereby opened the door for bigger wins by great Pekes to follow, ushering in the new era of the Pekingese superstar.

THE ERA OF THE PEKINGESE SUPERSTAR

In 1956 Jones and Taylor imported from England the Reserve CC winner, Ch. Chik T'Sun of Caversham, bred by Mary de Pledge and Herminie Lunham. After becoming Dog of the Year in Canada, Chik T'Sun was owned by Mr

and Mrs Charles Venable of Atlanta, Georgia, and was handled by one of the sport's most admired handlers, Clara Alford. Chik T'Sun went on to a legendary career, winning 169 Group Firsts, maintaining an all-time record of all breed Bests, winning the Toy Group at Westminster three times, then reaching the pinnacle of distinction by becoming the first Peke ever to win the coveted Westminster KC Best in Show. This was in 1960.

Chik T'Sun then made a lasting contribution to the North American gene pool through his top-quality progeny, such as his grand-daughter, Ch. St Aubrey Tinkabelle of Elsdon (by Mandarin), who was an excellent producer as well as a BIS winner and a PCA National Summer Specialty Best of Breed winner.

Ch. St Aubrey Tinkabelle Of Elsdon: BIS the Pekingese Club of America Summer Specialty. Photo: Shafer.

MOMENTOUS IMPACT

Back in 1960, when Chik T'Sun won BIS at Westminster, no one ever imagined that the best was yet to come. In 1975 Nigel Aubrey-Jones discovered a nine-month-old dog puppy in England who was in the ring with his breeder, Lilian Snook (Laparata), and persuaded Mrs Snook to allow him to buy the puppy. The history that followed had a momentous impact on the future of the breed in North America for the remainder of the century. The puppy was the great Ch. St Aubrey Laparata Dragon, who became a virtual legend in his own time,

Ch. St Aubrey Dragonora Of Elsdon: BIS Westminster KC 1982 – top winning bitch.

producing over 100 Champions, and ultimately carved his niche in history as the All Time Top Sire Of The Breed.

After Dragon's initial career in Canada, where he sired exceptionally well at the St Aubrey-Elsdon kennels, he was owned by Edward B. Jenner. Under the first-rate handling of Luc Boileau, Dragon had an extremely successful show career, winning numerous groups and all breed Bests in Show.

To Dragon's list of achievements must be added

that he produced not only top-notch Champions of recognizable type and quality, as well as progeny who would become top producers themselves, but above all he produced the top echelon of superstars, notably the unforgettably exquisite little 8-lb bitch, Ch. St Aubrey Dragonora of Elsdon, bred by Taylor and Jones, owned by Anne Snelling and handled throughout her illustrious career by William Trainor. In 1982 Dragonora became the second

Can. Ch. St Aubrey Dragonfly Of Elsdon: A leading sire and litter brother to Westminster BIS winner, Dragonara.

Ch. Morningstar Reverie: Group winner.

Pekingese in history to win Best in Show at Westminster, while her litter brother, Ch. St Aubrey Dragonfly of Elsdon, became one of the breed's most successful sires.

When Dragonfly was mated to his half-sister by Dragon, he produced one of his most influential sons, Ch. St Aubrey Sunburst of Elsdon, whose dam carried a line to the successful Pekehuis breeding of Ethel Partridge in England. Sunburst's breeding proved to be a crucial ingredient in the breed's modern development, as he is directly behind many of the top winning and producing dogs today, specifically through his three sons who have had a distinct influence on the breed: Ch. Briarcourt's Rule Britannia, Morningstar Sun King, and Ch. Hope's Firecracker Sparkler.

INFLUENTIAL STUD DOGS

Firecracker Sparkler was a successful show dog, bred and owned by long-time breeder, Hope Burghardt. He is currently behind some very successful

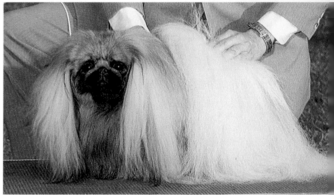

Ch. Morningstar Lionhart: Top sire, multiple Group winner.   *Photo: Graham.*

Ch. Morningstar Velvet Rose: The third bitch in history to win BIS at the Pekingese Club of America, and the first to win the Rotating National Specialty. Multiple Group 1 winner.

breeding, having sired many winners including BISA Ch. Hope's Merry Robin Hood as well as Cliff and Edie Jones' Group winning Ch. Lionshadow Prince Hilarion.

Another Sunburst son, Morningstar Sun King, a triple great-grandson of Dragon, became the foundation dog and an influential sire for the Morningstar breeding programme of John French and Anthony Rosato of Miami, Florida. Sun King sired top-quality progeny, including multiple Group winning Ch. Morningstar Lionhart who was a Top Sire, owned by Mrs R.I. Ballinger. Following down from Sun King are numerous linebred Morningstar Champions including three consecutive generations of all breed Best in Show winners, as well as the most recent Group winning Champion in direct line 10th generation descent from Sun King, Ch. Morningstar Reverie. Rosato and French also bred, owned and handled the multiple group winning bitch, Ch. Morningstar Velvet Rose, who in 1997 became the third bitch in history to win Best in Show at The Pekingese Club of America National Specialty.

The third influential Sunburst son, Ch. Briarcourt's Rule Britannia, carries Australian breeding through his dam's side, and, like his sire, became a pivotal dog in the development of the breed through the well-known Briarcourt kennel of Joan Mylchreest. Rule Britannia sired the top winning BIS and

Ch. Briarcourt's Damien Gable: Top Toy Dog, 1992 and 1993, twice Westminster Group 1 winner.

Ch. Briarcourt's Coral Gable: Westminster Group winner, all breed BIS winner, sire of Top Toy and many Champions.
Photo: Ashbey.

Westminster Group winner, Ch. Briarcourt's Coral Gable and is behind many Briarcourt Champions and top winning dogs today, including Coral Gable's famous top winning son, Ch. Briarcourt's Damien Gable who was Top Toy in the USA for 1992 and 1993 and a two-time Westminster Group winner. Coral Gable and his father were bred by one of America's leading breeders and top handlers, David Fitzpatrick. Another Rule Britannia son, who became the top winner on the West Coast, was named Ch. Briarcourt's Excelsior and was bred by Mrs Mylchreest, and owned by J. Robert Jacobsen.

Rule Britannia also sired the famous Ch. Wendessa Crown Prince, who was Top Toy in America in 1989 and became the third Peke in history to win Best In Show at Westminster in 1990. Crown Prince, who was bred by Mrs Ronald Bramson, owned by Edward B. Jenner and handled by Luc Boileau, then scored another great achievement in the breed by siring one of the most successful sires in history, Ch. Knolland Red Rover.

Ch. Knolland Red Rover: BIS winner, top sire for many years.   *Photo: Alex Smith.*

Ch. Akarana Excalibur: Winner of ten all breed BIS and Groups firsts. Photo: Dee.

Ch. St Aubrey Bon Jovi of Elsdon: Westminster Best of Breed winner, National Specialty BIS.

CH. KNOLLAND RED ROVER

Red Rover is a very linebred dog, who, in addition to being a grandson of the prepotent Dragon, has another five crosses to Dragon within five generations. He was bred by Edward B. Jenner and is owned by Michael Hill of Toronto. Like his grandfather, Rover has also proven to be an extremely valuable prepotent sire. With the number of winners and Champions still climbing, so far Rover has produced more than 87 Champions, 11 of which are BIS winners, with 25 offspring winning Group Firsts, including Ch. Akarana Excalibur who was Top Pekingese in America, bred by Michael Hill, owned and handled by Gareth Morgan-Jones and Richard Albee.

Another Rover son, Ch. St Aubrey Bon Jovi of Elsdon, was a Westminster Best of Breed winner and a National

Int. Ch. Rodari Orient Express.
Photo: Bergman.

Specialty BIS winner, owned by Laura Carlstrom, Jean Pennel, Mary Schuyler Campbell, Dale Martensen, and Molly Bustin.

Ch. Lorricbrook Waldo The Great, bred by Canadian breeder/judge Max Magder and owned by Ingela Gram, is a Red Rover son who is a Group and all

Above: Ch. Rodari The Dragon At Lon-Du: Leading sire handled by owner Arlon Duit

Left: Ch. Rodari Aces High with his breeder, Mrs Barbara Mellis. No. 1 Peke in Canada and winner of 50 all breed BISs. Photo: Alex Smith.

breed BIS winner who further distinguished himself by winning BIS at the 1998 Rotating National Specialty.

Yet another Red Rover son, of international renown and influence, is Int. Ch. Rodari Orient Express, bred by Barbara Mellis in Canada, and now owned by Michael Tong in Hong Kong. Orient Express became a important sire in the UK and Asia and has had a considerable influence in the gene pool worldwide. Barbara Mellis' Rodari kennel has been noted for many winning Champions over the years, including the recent big winner, Ch.

Rodari Aces High, winner of 50 all breed BIS including Canada's prestigious Show of Shows, as well as numerous specialties. Mrs Mellis is also the breeder of one of America's most popular top sires, a dog who produced many big winners, the closely linebred Dragon grandson, Ch. Rodari The Dragon at Lon-Du, owned by Arlon Duit of Monticello, Iowa, another of America's top breeders.

MODERN HISTORY

If we consider the impact on the breed of the many great winners and

*Ch. St Aubrey Bees Wing of
Elsdon: Top Toy Dog 1985.*

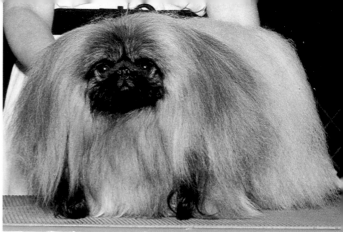

*Ch. St Aubrey
Domingo of Elsdon.*

producers since 1975, we can see that
the modern history of the North
American Pekingese has been shaped by
the emergence of one particularly gifted
stud dog, Ch. St Aubrey Laparata
Dragon. As a sure testimony to
successful linebreeding, it is clear that
Dragon's prepotency as a sire has been
reliable and traceable through many
generations, with sons, daughters and
grandchildren on down bearing the
quality of his lineage.

CHAMPION PROGENY

Of all the Champion progeny of
Dragon's, perhaps the most famous of
his sons was Ch. St Aubrey Bees Wing
of Elsdon, also owned by Edward B.
Jenner and handled by Luc Boileau.
Bees Wing became Top Toy Dog in the
American show ring in 1986, and was a
successful sire as well. Bees Wing's
grandson, Ch. St Aubrey Pavarotti of
Elsdon became America's No. 1
Pekingese in 1995 and the No. 9 Toy
for owners, Edie and Cliff Jones,
handled by Brenda Scheiblauer.

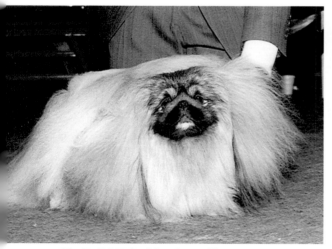

*Ch. Jo-Li Wind in the Willows:
Top winner and influential sire.*

*Ch. Reedmar Power Broker:
Top Pekingese 1994.*

Pavarotti's full brother, Ch. St Aubrey Domingo of Elsdon, also became a BIS winner for Edie Jones, both dogs' parents being the well-known top producers, Ch. St Aubrey Chit Chat of Elsdon and Ch. St Aubrey Melba of Elsdon, a Bees Wing daughter.

Bees Wing's famous winning son, Ch. Jo-Li Wind In The Willows, bred and owned by another respected breeder/exhibitor of several breeds Joseph F. Joly III, became one of the breed's top show dogs, winning many Groups and BIS as well as Best of Breed at Westminster and going on to have a

Ch. Masterpiece Zodiac of Dud-Lees: Multiple BIS all breeds, pictured with breeder Ruby Dudley.

considerable influence on the American Pekingese gene pool.

Wind In The Willows came from a litter of four sired by Bees Wing out of Ch. Dud-Lees Fancy Love Affair. All four of the siblings became easy Champions. All looked remarkably similar with very short bodies, exceptionally long coats and expressive heads.

One of the litter brothers, Ch. Jo-Li Virtuous Dragon, also became an all breed Best in Show winner, and then sired Ch. Reedmar Power Broker who became Top Pekingese in 1994 and won BIS at The Pekingese Club of America National Specialty. Power Broker is bred and owned by Margaret and Patricia Reed and Joy Brewster.

DUD-LEES

It is important to note that the breeder of the dam of the above-mentioned litter of four is Ruby Dudley (Dud-Lees) of Creston, Iowa, who has bred 126 Champions. Most of Dud-Lees breeding goes back to two important sires acquired from the successful California breeder, Irene Ruschaupt, named Int. Ch. Ku-Chin Tom-mi of Seng Kye, who was a Best in Show winner, and his son, Ch. Tommi Masterpiece Sing Lee. Tommi, in turn, produced Ch. Zodiac Masterpiece of Dud-Lees, who had a flourishing career under the ownership of another famous partnership, that of Mrs Walter M. Jeffords and Michael Wolf.

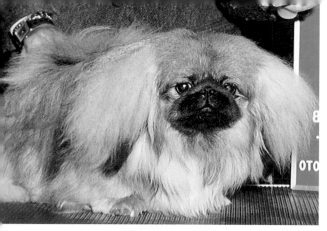

Ch. Chico of Chinatown:
PCA BIS winter Specialty.

Ch. Shinnecock of Chinatown: Twice winner
of the Pekingese Club of America Winter
Specialty; Westminster BOB winner.

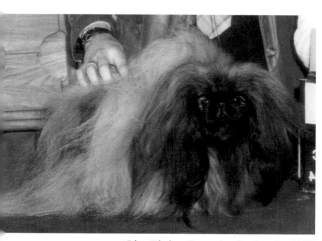

Ch. Elpha-Sun Arrhythmia: BIS
Specialty winning bitch, 10 Group 1s.

WOLF AND JEFFORDS

The Wolf and Jeffords team was one of the most successful in modern breed history, with several top-quality dogs reaching their highest potential under the partnership's guidance, beginning with British import Ch. Dagbury of Calartha, who began his American career winning Best in Show from the classes. Some of the great show dogs jointly owned by Mrs Jeffords and Mr Wolf were: Ch. Quilkin The Stringman, who won Best of Breed at The Pekingese Club of America National Specialty three times, along with 11 BIS all breeds, and Ch. Yankee Bernard, a Westminster Toy Group winner and a PCA Best of Breed winner with at least 17 all breed Bests in Show.

In the 1980s Mrs Jeffords developed an extensive Pekingese breeding programme, which produced a steady stream of Champions and top winners, all of similar exceptional type and quality, such as Ch. Chico of Chinatown, who won Best in Show at the Pekingese Club of America in 1987. One of the most successful dogs bred by Mrs Jeffords was Ch. Shinnecock of Chinatown, a Westminster Best of Breed winner and twice Best of Breed at the PCA winter Specialty in New York. He was sired by the Ch. Shiarita Cassidy son, Eng. Am. Ch. Belknap Kalafrana Caspar, owned by Augusta Maynard of Southampton, NY.

Caspar also sired the popular top winning bitch owned by Mrs Maynard, and handled by William Trainor, known as Ch. Velspring Velvetina. Like the famous Westminster BIS winning Dragonora, Velvetina underscored America's love for small glamorous bitches as she piloted herself to top ratings.

DOLL-MCGINNIS

Another bitch who captured the hearts of many was the ultra-glamorous Best in Specialty winning, Ch. Elpha-Sun Arrhythmia, a winner of over 40 Group placements and 10 Group Firsts. Arrhythmia was bred, owned and handled by Joe McGinnis and Duane Doll from Lakeland, Florida, who have bred and exhibited numerous Champions for many years, including Group and all breed BIS winners. The Doll-McGinnis partnership hosts the annual Black Masked Ball which kicks

Ch. Cambalu Hurly Burly: One of the winning Cambalu bitches.

Ch. Hope's Dash of Eberhard: One of the top winning blacks in history.

Ch. Lakshmi Valentino of Jo-Li: Top Pekingese 1998.

off the first evening's festivities during the Rotating Pekingese Club of America National Specialty.

HOPE AND PAUL BURGHARDT

Today there are a number of excellent Pekingese breeders who are making their mark on the breed, and clearly two of the most successful are Hope and Paul Burghardt of Mirador Farm in Virginia. Originally established in St Louis, Missouri, Hope's breeding is based on Miralac, Appin, St Aubrey-Elsdon, Cambalu, Morningstar, Ai Kou, Claymore, Briarcourt and Mahjon, with the British Mahjon breeding coming as a result of Pat Drew's four-year residence in Columbus, Indiana, where she lived with 10 Pekes, all of which she brought with her from her native England, and mostly of Belknap and Shiarita breeding.

Hope Burghardt also had a strong association with the successful breeder Marjorie B. (Kaye) Cooke in St Louis. The latter's Cambalu breeding (later in partnership with Richard Kruger) was noted for exquisite, top-quality bitches and produced some of the most influential dogs to affect the North American gene pool. These include Ch. Cambalu Sunstorm who produced many winners, and Cambalu King Bee Morningstar who is repeated in many pedigrees worldwide, as well as the beautiful winning bitch, Ch. Cambalu Hurly Burly. Other notable Cambalu influences are the bitches, Ch. Cambalu Sunburst Serena (a Sunburst daughter), Ch. Cambalu King's Court Mandolin, Cambalu Queenie Bee and Ch. Cambalu Wee Sed T'Ruffles.

Always an extremely dedicated breeder, Hope, along with her husband Paul, have had several top winning dogs, from Firecracker Sparkler to the Best in Show winning black dog, Ch. Hope's Dash of Eberhard, to the Westminster Best of Breed winner, Ch. Hope's Merry Robin Hood, handled by Greg Robinson. Ch. Pequest Picasso became the next big winner for the Burghardts, bred by their handler, David Fitzpatrick, and was campaigned to No. 1 Peke in America. Picasso was also twice winner of The Pekingese Club of America National Specialty, has numerous Group Firsts and BIS and is siring top-quality progeny, such as the Specialty and Group winning Ch. Hope's Don Juan of Mirador.

In 1998 the No.1 Peke in the US and No.2 Toy was another of the Burghardts' great winners, named Ch. Lakshmi Valentino of Jo-Li, bred by Irene Reasons and Joseph Joly III. Valentino gained his title winning all breed BIS from the classes, and amassed a terrific record of Group and BIS wins. Valentino's co-breeder, Irene Reasons (Lakshmi), in Hartwell, Georgia, is another of America's leading breeders and has produced many notable Champions over the years. In partnership with Mr Joly, Irene co-bred another all breed BIS winner, Ch. Jo-Li

163

Ch. Windemere's Peter Piper Sing Lee (left) and Ch. Morningstar Festival Music: Two top winning Pekes. *Photo: Booth.*

Ch. Claymore Summer Smoke: Multiple Group winner. *Photo: Ashbey.*

Ch. Santaverdi Wise Guy: Group and Specialty winner. *Photo: Olson.*

Rufus of Lakshmi, owned by Mrs Jerry Gray of Alvin, Texas.

BREED INFLUENCES BY REGION
THE SOUTHERN UNITED STATES

All throughout the various regions of North America, there are key breeder/exhibitors whose efforts and experience are having an important influence on the growth and development of the breed. In the Southern US, Herb and Erna

Holcombe of the Lin-Lee Pekingese in Morris, Alabama, have had considerable success with several top winning Pekes, including their homebred BISA Ch. Linn-Lee's Royal Silberman, followed by Ch. Windemere's Peter Piper Sing Lee and Ch. Morningstar Festival Music. Peter Piper was the 1997 Westminster Best of Breed winner and a top-rated Peke with multiple Group Firsts and all breed BIS, while Festival Music has numerous group wins and was No.2 Peke in the USA throughout 1998.

Also in Alabama, top breeder/exhibitors Mike Moore and David Bowman have campaigned many winners, including Ch. Etive Nutcracker and Ch. Merrimac Andreas Silberman, as well as having shared in the campaign of Peter Piper. Nearby in Auburn, Alabama, Gareth Morgan-Jones and Richard Albee have developed a successful programme which is home to a number of imports and Champions including their top winner, Ch. Akarana Excalibur, a No. 1 Peke who ended his career with 10 all breed Bests in Show and 60 Toy Group Firsts.

Though originally from the Northeast, today Mrs Robert I. Ballinger (Claymore) is one of the breed's long-time top breeder/exhibitors, residing with her Pekes in Palm Beach, Florida for eight months of the year and in New

Hampshire during the summer. Among Mrs Ballinger's many well-known winners are BIS Ch. Claymore's Cinnamon Bun, and group winners Ch. Knolland Slowboat To China, Ch. Morningstar Lionhart, plus the group winning bitch, Ch. Claymore Delphinium and her son, Ch. Claymore Storm Warning, the No.5 Pekingese for 1997. In recent years the glamorous group winning homebred, Ch. Claymore Summer Smoke, maintained himself in the top ratings, handled by Bill Trainor, while the newest homebred is the Pavarotti son, Claymore Opening Night, who is a group winner while still a puppy. There have been numerous Claymore Champions over the years, and the breeding from this long-established kennel has proved to be an important influence in several successful breeding programmes throughout the US and Canada.

Among the many other successful breeder/exhibitors in the South are:

Ch. Carr's Top Brass: All breed and Specialty BIS winner, pictured with judge Anthony Rosato, owner Ky Oulay and longtime breeder Peggy Dillard Carr.

Photo: Sosa.

Int. Ch. Rosayleen The Gaffer At Sunsalve.

Ch. Jo-Li Rufus of Lakshmi: All breed BIS winner. Photo: Petrulis.

Larry Elks (Elksway) who has had many successful dogs including the big winner, Ch. Elksway Entertainer; Frank Tingley (Ly-Ton); Bert Jacques (Ja-Lar); Don Johnson (Peh-Kai); Carole Noe and Leone Kneibusch (Shenblu); Diane Tredwell (Purdue Place); Jeanette Franklin (Corralitos); and J. Ann Vincent (Taralon).

In Tennessee, Peggy Dillard Carr and her husband, Houston, have been active breeders for some 45 years, and have had a number of outstanding dogs of exceptional type and quality. One of the Carrs' homebreds, Ch. Carr's Top Brass, has multiple all breed BIS, specialty Bests and many groups wins to his credit.

Kathy and Tom Masilla of Metarie, Louisiana, are also long-time dedicated breeders, who have incorporated breeding from top American, Canadian and British kennels under their Santaverdi affix, and have frequently had dogs in the Top Ten over the years, such as all breed BIS winners Ch. Santaverdi The Wise Guy, and Ch. St Aubrey Jeeves of Elsdon.

Then, too, the great Lone Star State of Texas has been home to many influential and successful breeders, from Mrs Murray Brooks and her Caversham-based Tien Hai Pekingese to Ruby Turner Williams whose He-Lo Pekingese were the basis of several successful breeding programs over the years, including Mrs Metzger's Muhlins, the Chambrae Pekingese of Christine Hann, and Cleda Olsen's Shady Acres Pekingese. During the 1970s and 80s breeder/judges, Don Sutton and Steve Keating (Sutton Place) had at least 30 Champions, many homebred and owner-handled. Sutton and Keating also imported dogs from England, and certainly none more famous than Int. Ch. Rosayleen The Gaffer at Sunsalve who was Top Pekingese in the UK and a multiple all breed BIS winner in America. Among the top breeder/exhibitors in recent years in Texas are Annette Borders (Honeybear) who has had many glamorous winners; Sam and Marilyn Dudley (Sa-Du); Marion Gipson (Blossomtel); Gloria Blum (Gee-Gee); as well as Jerry Gray

166

(DJ), who has had many big winners such as Ch. Jo-Li Rufus of Lakshmi, plus England's Top Pekingese Ch. St Sanja Star Attraction of Genderlee, and her multi-BIS specialty winner, Ch. Morningstar City Lights.

Ch. Briarcourt's Excelsior: Top winner on the West Coast in the 1980s.   Photo: Callea

THE WESTERN UNITED STATES

West Coast breeders Joy Thoms (Windemere) and Janet and J. Robert Jacobsen (Sing-Lee) are co-breeders of one of the top winning Pekes in the US, Ch. Windermere's Peter Piper Sing Lee. The Jacobsens have had numerous top winning group and BIS winning Pekes for many years, and both husband and wife are active multi-breed judges. One of their early favourite big winners was Ch. California Gold Sing Lee, who had an impressive record on the West Coast with multiple groups, specialty and all breed Bests. The Jacobsens also won BIS at PCA with Ch. Raffles Jubilation Sing Lee, a multiple group and specialty winner. In the 1980s the Jacobsens owned and campaigned the famous Rule Britannia son, Ch. Briarcourt's Excelsior, who was one of the nation's top winners, ending his career with 13 all breed BIS, as well as 79 Group Firsts and four specialty Bests. Bob and Janet have also had a much success with the two group winning littermates to Peter Piper, Ch. Windemere's Peter Pan Sing Lee and Ch. Windemere's Gold Fever Sing Lee, the latter being a PCA National Specialty winner in 1995. The three winning littermates were sired by

Ch. Windemere's Gold Fever Sing Lee: National Specialty BIS winner.

Ch. Windemere's Hard to be Humble.

167

Ch. Ai Kou Sunni Dragon: ten Groups 1s, multiple BISS winner, leading sire.

Ch. Mei Li Masquerade: A leading sire.

Ch. Ai Kou Weekend Warrior: 27 Group 1s, multiple BIS Specialty winner.

Ch. Draco's Mystical Rhapsody: BIS Specialty winning daughter of Ch. Knolland Red Rover.

all breed BIS winner, Ch. Yakee A Town Called Malice, a double Ch. Shiarita Cassidy grandson, owned by Litha McPherson of Aldergrove, British Columbia, Canada.

In Oregon, Joy Thoms' breeding has been a valuable asset to many breeding programmes for a long time, having served as the basis for other kennels' success and offering popular dogs at stud, including Ch. Windermere's Hard To Be Humble, who Joy handled herself to a number of impressive wins. Joy is also one of the leading breeders of quality white Pekes, and continues to devote her efforts and long-term goals to raising the standard of quality in white Pekes for present and future generations.

In California, the famous Ai Kou kennel of Jean Thomas has long been regarded as one of the leading forces in the American Peke world. The Ai Kou Pekingese have had 145 Champions of which many were famous winners, including Ch. Cherangani Bombardier and Ch. Ai Kou Sunni Dragon, an excellent producer and son of the famous Ch. St Aubrey Laparata Dragon. Today the kennel continues in the forefront of success, kept on course by Mrs Thomas' former handler and daughter-in-law, Lois Frank Thomas, whose breeding has produced such noted winners as Ch. Ai Kou Weekend Warrior (27 Group Firsts, 4 BISS) co-owned by Barbara Verzi, Ch. Ai Kou Chances Are (6 BISS, 12 Group Firsts) and Ch. Ai Kou Easy Chances (BISS, 6 Group Firsts). Additionally, Ai Kou breeding has ultimately served as the foundation for many successful breeding programmes in the US.

California has many successful breeders whose efforts have played an important role in the development of the breed. In the San Francisco area, Lucille Tulloch (Mei Li) has incorporated breeding from top UK kennels, such as Laparata, Belknap, Lotusgrange and Shiarita, and has produced many beautiful winners for many years, including one of the breed's best sires, Ch. Mei Li Masquerade. Jackie Ragland (Ja-Ling) has also produced many winning dogs and is the owner of 1993 PCA BIS winner, Ch. Taeplace Tabasco of Ja-Ling, bred by Canadians Beth and John Ferrier. Jim King (King's Court) had great success with his homebred Ch. King's Court Social Lion, who was Top Pekingese and BIS at the Pekingese Club of America. Social Lion in turn sired the top winning Ch. Pequest Picasso as well as eleven more Champions. Paul and

Pam Winters (Draco) did extremely well with the glamorous Red Rover daughter, BISS Ch. Draco's Mystical Rhapsody, who won consistently well in every part of the continent where she was shown and went on to produce winning progeny. Also, the long-time successful Dragonhai kennel of Hal Fraser and Allen Williams has been noted for its typical, glamorous Pekes and enjoyed success in the early 1990s with Ch. Sunsante Prince Henry At Dragonhai. Other West Coast breeders such as Chuck and Kim Langley (Cee-Kae), Jim and Cheryl Yeager (Jir-Cen), Tula Damon (Finnfair), Ed Doroliat and Ernie Camisa (La Conquette) and Rod Chu (Zitan) have dedicated and progressive breeding programmes and are producing quality, winning Pekingese.

SOUTH WEST
In the Southwestern US, it has been breeders such as Lynn and Mal Simpson (Sai Chi), Joe and Jean Hileman (Desert Jade), and Sandy Wheat (Mugiechun) among others, who have made valuable contributions to the Pekingese gene pool.

PACIFIC NORTHWEST
In the Pacific Northwest, Greg Robinson is a breeder/exhibitor who has had outstanding successes in the ring with many top winning Group and BIS dogs. In the same region, Bobbie Fraser (Fraser-Manor) has been a long-

time fancier since the 1940s and produced many Champions. It is also very encouraging that a newer generation of breeders, such as David T. Huynh (Purling Mists) in Seattle, are bringing their enthusiasm to the breed and are having success in the ring.

THE NORTHEASTERN UNITED STATES

In the early part of the 20th century, the hub of breeding and show-related activity was the Northeast, where The Pekingese Club of America was deeply rooted and many of the country's most prestigious shows were held. Some of the early influential kennels were located in this region, including Mrs Quigley's famous Orchard Hill dogs and John B. Royce's Dah-Lyn winners, to more modern influences such as Ho Dynasty (G. Blauvelt-Moss and J. Goble), Mike-Mar (Michael Wolf), Chinatown (Kathleen Jeffords) and Briarcourt (Joan Mylchreest). The Northeast continues to be a region of important influence, with such long-time breeders as Pat and Charles Farley (Chu Lai) and Betty Tilley (Pleiku) who are both breeders of consistent quality. Also, Mona Fosella (Of The Gorge) produced many winning dogs including an all breed BIS winner. Tony and Judy Pomato (Wun Chun) are both highly respected for their top quality, as are Edie and Cliff Jones (Lionshadow) who have bred several Champions and have campaigned all breed BIS winners

including the Top Peke. Mrs Ronald Bramson (Wendessa) is the breeder of a National Specialty BIS winning bitch, Ch. Lady Farrah of Fourwinds, and the famous Westminster BIS winner, Crown Prince. Also in the Northeast, Sally Hestle is dedicated to maintaining Briarcourt breeding, as is David Fitzpatrick, while Pat and Harry Harrison (Showtime) are known for their success with BIS and specialty winners, and Claudia Covo (Qui Chang) has kept her group winning parti-colors in the limelight.

RUTHE PAINTER

When we are talking about contributions of great people in the breed, one cannot underestimate the effect that Pennsylvania breeder, Ruthe Painter, had on the breed for a long time. Not only did she have a good deal of success in all breed competition with her numerous Champions, group and BIS winning Pekingese exclusively handled by Elaine Rigden for 17 years, such as Ch. Oakmere The Baron and Ch. Lotusgrange Another Venture, but it was Ruthe's vision of annually uniting breeders from every region in the country on a large scale for competition and camaraderie which ultimately became the springboard for initiating the Rotating National Specialty in 1990 which has had a greatly beneficial effect on the breed as a whole.

THE MIDWESTERN UNITED STATES

Anyone studying Pekingese pedigrees will surely recognize that a high percentage of influential sires and dams from the 1970s onward came from or through Midwest kennels. Without question, one of the foremost influences from this region is Edward B. Jenner's

Ch. Fourwinds Princely Pearl: 200th Champion for Mr and Mrs R.M. Jackson. Photo: Booth.

Ch. Belknap Little Nugget.

and Luc Boileau's Knolland Farm, which has long been home to top winning dogs of many breeds, including two Westminster BIS winners, the Standard Poodle, Ch. Acadia's Command Performance, and the Pekingese, Ch. Wendessa Crown Prince. Clearly, when history takes a retrospective look at the progress North American Pekingese have made in the last half of the 20th century, Jenner's and Boileau's contribution to the breed comes into sharpest focus, not just for the distinguished roster of stars which have come through Knolland Farm, maintaining the breed's prestige in the dog show community. Equally important are the many influential dogs owned by or bred at Knolland Farm which can be found in pedigrees all throughout North America, including the two most famous prepotent sires in the breed's North American history, Ch. St Aubrey Laparata Dragon and Ch. Knolland Red Rover.

In Illinois, Bob and Mary Ann Jackson have the world-renowned Fourwinds Pekingese which have been in existence since the 1950s. The Jacksons have had well over 220 Champions, including group winners, regional and national specialty winners, and have supplied dedicated breeders with quality breeding stock and Champions for decades. They have imported extensively from the UK and are one of the few large-scale breeding kennels of Pekingese show stock in America.

Also in Illinois, Patricia Metzger's Muhlin Pekingese have been a major influence in the Pekingese gene pool in North America since 1970. She has owned or bred 45 Champions and has made available top producing dogs at stud, such as Ch. Belknap Little Nugget and Ch. Muhlin Boogaloo, the latter being co-owned with Christine Hann (Chambrae), another noted breeder who has made a name with her winning blacks.

Many other successful breeders, who support the region's breed clubs, have also made valuable contributions to the breed in recent years, such as Jerelyn Atwell-Paul and Barbara Maske (Nevon), Roger and Judy Sankey (Sanrae), Jan Felkamp (Chin Tse), Roger and Lina de La Paz (Emerlins), Bert and Don Custudio (Tradewinds), Barbara Stremke (Prima) and the successful family team, Larry, DeAnn, Jason and Chad Ulmer (Prairie Breeze), who have owned and bred all breed BIS winners, including multiple BIS Ch. Morningstar Monte Carlo, his son BIS Ch. Prairie Breeze Can't Touch This, and the newest big winner, Ch. Prairie Breeze Boogie Woogie.

MORE CANADIAN INFLUENCE

In Canada, apart from the well-known leading kennels of St Aubrey-Elsdon, Rodari, Manticore and Akarana, which have had long histories of success, there are several more Canadian breeders whose efforts have produced winning dogs which are an important influence on the breed. Rena Dee Dee Jones (Cinnabar) and Max Magder (Lorricbrook) have both produced all breed BIS winners. Since the 1970s, the Saimaifun Pekingese of Doug and Diane Kleinsorge of Vancouver, B.C., have had many glamorous Jamestown-descended Champions. Also to the fore are Brian and Shealah McClelland (Briobar), John and Beth Ferrier (Taeplace), Gail Forsythe (Lionheart), Margaret Roberge (Lawbugtee), Lois McIntosh (Pagoda Place), Gary Tucker (Michaelmas), Michael Guy (Leachim), Melody Gault (Dachari), Danny Detonnancour (Weitoi), Marthe Baizana (Baizana) and many others, each committed to developing the breed and many of whom have produced top quality specimens.

A RICH HISTORY

The Pekingese in North America has indeed enjoyed a rich history of growth and success throughout the entire 20th century. And, as the dog show sport itself keeps growing, changing, improving, the Pekingese breed shows every sign of keeping pace. Building on the foundation laid by those long devoted to the breed, the Pekingese breeders and exhibitors of tomorrow are supported by a great legacy, and can look to the breed's future with enthusiasm and great opportunity.

11 *PEKINGESE WORLDWIDE*

Although the breed originated in China, during the time of the Cultural Revolution when the country was closed off to the outside world, Pekingese and all other domestic animals disappeared.

As people were struggling to feed themselves and their children, obviously there was no place for dogs.

In the 1980's dogs started being taken into the country in small numbers mainly with overseas Embassy staff.

There have been some show dogs and breeding stock sent to China from Hong Kong but the situation is still very precarious as dogs are still illegal in Beijing and there is no Kennel Club or official body to deal with pedigrees etc.

HONG KONG

In Hong Kong there has been a strong dog show scene for many years and the Hong Kong Kennel Club is recognised by the English Kennel Club. Pekingese have been some of the most prolific

winners at Hong Kong shows and the CC record holder is a Pekingese.

Hong Kong Ch. Lotusgrange Fine Venture, a Yu Yang grandson, was imported by Maria Francis in the early seventies after she moved back to Hong Kong taking the nucleus of her kennel with her which was mostly Welion breeding.

He won Reserve BIS at the 1976 All Breeds Championship show and was the sire of the first Cisfran champion who was also the first Peke bitch Champion.

The kennel then based its breeding programme on Shiarita, and Shiarita The First Mate won Reserve BIS in 1990 followed by Ch. Yakee Here's

HK Ch. Yakee Here's Looking At You: Reserve BIS Hong Kong Championship Show 1992 and 1998.

HK Ch. Tilouet Spun Silk: BIS in 1993. This is a Cassidy daughter out of a Fort Lauderdale daughter. Her litter sister is the dam of Goodall's Siver Queen.

Looking At You in 1992, 1998 and BIS in 1993. He was a Cassidy grandson and in 1993 a Cassidy daughter Tilouet Spun Silk won BIS to date the only bitch to achieve this high award in Hong Kong. Her dam was a Fort Lauderdale daughter and her unshown litter sister was the dam of Tilouet Silver Queen At Shihgo, the breed's top brood bitch in the United Kingdom.

In 1992 Maria Francis formed the international kennel Franshaw with John Shaw, a long time Peke fancier. Purchasing the English Champion, Shiarita Emperor Roscoe winner of BOB Crufts 1994, they campaigned him internationally with great success. He gained his titles in America, Canada and Holland and won two BIS in Hong Kong gaining his Asian title before retiring to live as Mr Shaw's companion. His son, Asian Champion

Ph. Ch. Dreamville Sun Goddess winning Best Puyppy at her first American show.

Rickshaw Count Basie, has twice won Res. BIS in 1997 and 1998.

Roscoe has sired Champions in each of the countries he has lived in and the Cisfran/Franshaw kennels have, between them, accounted for ten of the seventeen Pekingese Champions ever made up in Hong Kong.

PHILIPPINES

Another eastern country that has a strong Peke influence is the Phillippines where Dr Raymond Lo has the Dreamville Pekes.

Dr Lo and his wife, both pathologists, returned to the Philippines in 1987 from America with two bitches from the Fourwinds kennel. From one of these they produced Philippines Champion Dreamville Just A Fantasy who became a BIS winner.

They imported stock from Shiarita in the United Kingdom, St Aubrey Eldson (Canada) and Morning Star (US) and soon became the top winning kennel. In partnership with American breeders they have bred four American Champions.

One of his main winners is American champion D Sun Godess who the day after she and her breeder had made the

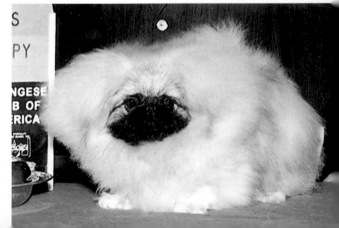

Int. Ch. Pekellen Chi-Chi With Oakmere, owned by Bianca Scheira (Switzerland).

eighteen hour trip to New York at seven months old, won Best Sweepstakes and Best Puppy in show under noted breeders Irene Reasons and Michael Hill. She quickly became a champion and her breeding combines Shiarita (she is a descendant of Ch. Shiarita Bobby Dazzler) and St Aubrey.

HOLLAND

In Europe one of the main Pekingese kennels must be that of the Eastcourts owned by Letty and Dick Oosterhof. They started breeding in 1968 and have imported many dogs from England, mainly Jamestown descendants, to produce thirty-four Dutch Champions. To make a Champion in Holland requires winning four C.A.C.I.B. the last of which must be won after the dog is twenty seven months old, which can be difficult with bitches coming in season and losing their coats.

They have won over 250 CACIBs and numerous Toy Groups, with dogs such as Ch. Fu-Yang Of Lotusgrange, English and Dutch Champion Shiarita San Francisco, and Ch. Royceland Moonglow Of Shiarita.

Ch. Sandokan Of Eastcourt was one of their earlier big winners, winning BIS in 1979. They owned or bred the World Champion of 1973, Champion Suzie Wong Of E, Chantal Of E and Shiarita Las Vegas in 1980, plus the Las Vegas litter brother and sister, The Proof and All In One in 1985.

The Dutch show of Crufts is the Amsterdam Winners and the Eastcourt kennel have been winners here over twenty-five times.

The Toy Dog Club gives its own title as it is an important Championship show and all of the previously mentioned dogs have been club winners as well as Shiarita Fort Edditson who won this title in 1993.

Their most recent winners have been the half brother sons of Roscoe, Illegal Romeo Of E. who was a Club winner in 1997 and is now an American Champion. Ch. Stand Up Comedian Of E. was an Amsterdam Youth Winner in 1997 and a Club Winner in 1998. He won the CACIB and BOB who at the Winners Show in 1998 and went on to win the Toy Group.

NORWAY

One of a number of kennels in Norway is that of Lily Froyland who has based her line on Singlewell and is a frequent visitor to English shows. Her Norwegian Champion S. Hey Yu is a son of Wee Sedso, and sire of Norway and Finnish Champion Ching-Mei's Taj Prince and his brother Norway and Swedish Champion Blake Carrington. She also owned English Ch. Singlewell Magic Charm whom she campaigned to her international title and who was Top Peke in Norway in 1986. Her later Champion Ruling Emperor Of S. was a son of S. Magic Ruler.

The top winning Toy dog in Norway in 1987 was the Pekingese Nor. Sw. Ch. Royceland Lapaloma For Toydom owned by Bonny Sorenson, who not only is a frequent visitor to the UK but judged a Championship Show here in 1997.

Lapaloma went on to Top Dog All Breeds in 1989 following in the steps of his kennelmate Int. Ch. Sunsalve Come Play With Me At Toydom who was Top Dog in 1982.

The Hotpoint kennel have had over fifty Norwegian Champions in Pekingese. Her other breed, Great Danes, have been very successful in Scandinavia and four imports have become English Champions.

DENMARK

Marie Petersen of the KISCI kennel has had a number of homebred champions and travels to many European countries winning multiple titles on her dogs. She imported Fine Fella Of Lotusgrange with ICC and six reserve CCs and he soon became a Champion and world winner.

FINLAND

A relatively young kennel, Backlee, owned by Pia Backman has had some success mainly based on her original imports from Rosayleen. Her homebred male Finland and Est. Ch. Backlee The Body Guard was Top Peke in 1996 and 1997.

GERMANY

Suntoy is owned by another young lady Gabriele Runge, who campaigns her dogs in Europe with success. She has made up Champions in Luxembourg, Holland, Switzerland, Denmark and Belgium. Dam of two of her big winners was Highmead Pippin At Oakmere, an English import.

There are many more Pekingese lovers worldwide but, because of the British quarantine laws, we do not have the chance to compete in their own countries. Some of them come to England to see our shows and buy stock and we enjoy exchanging ideas and learning from each other.

Through our love of Pekes, we all have friends worldwide, and even with language difficulties we communicate with each other about our Oriental canine friends.